Transatlantic traumas

D1568873

MANCHESTER
1824
Manchester University Press

POCKET POLITICS

SERIES EDITOR: BILL JONES

Pocket politics presents short, pithy summaries of complex topics on socio-political issues both in Britain and overseas. Academically sound, accessible and aimed at the interested general reader, the series will address a subject range including political ideas, economics, society, the machinery of government and international issues. Unusually, perhaps, authors are encouraged, should they choose, to offer their own conclusions rather than strive for mere academic objectivity. The series will provide stimulating intellectual access to the problems of the modern world in a user-friendly format.

Previously published
The Trump revolt   Edward Ashbee
Lobbying: An appraisal   Wyn Grant
Power in modern Russia: Strategy and mobilisation
Andrew Monaghan
Reform of the House of Lords   Philip Norton
Government by referendum   Matt Qvortrup

Transatlantic traumas
Has illiberalism brought the West to the brink of collapse?

Stanley R. Sloan

Manchester University Press

Published by Manchester University Press
Altrincham Street, Manchester M1 7JA

www.manchesteruniversitypress.co.uk

British Library Cataloguing-in-Publication Data
A catalogue record for this book is available from the British Library

ISBN   978 1 5261 2871 3   paperback

First published 2018

Typeset by
Servis Filmsetting Ltd, Stockport, Cheshire
Printed in Great Britain by
CPI Group (UK) Ltd, Croydon CR0 4YY

Contents

Acknowledgments

I am endlessly thankful for my association with Middlebury College and its marvelous students for the inspirations and challenges they have provided over the past fourteen years of teaching in the Winter Term. This project owes much to three former students in my Euro-Atlantic Relations course – Rowen Price, Travis Sanderson and Grace Vedock – who volunteered to serve as research assistants and became full-fledged collaborators. I benefited as well from dialogues with Lawrence Chalmer, Jordan Becker, Thomas Seifert, Tom Timberman and my book club colleagues, who have added wise counsel on many issues addressed in this volume. It has been a pleasure working with Bill Jones, the editor of this series, and with Tony Mason and the rest of the team at Manchester University Press. Finally, my loving wife Monika once again provided not only eagle-eyed proofreading but also great patience with an author frequently lost in thought. As always, I am solely responsible for any errors of omission or commission.

Stanley R. Sloan, Lake Groton, Vermont

Introduction: the West, its ideas and enemies

> The West of which we speak is defined by the values of liberal democracy, individual freedom, human rights, tolerance and equality under the rule of law.

The most difficult part of solving a problem often is defining it. Only in the past few years has it become clear that what we call "the West" has become vulnerable to a potent combination of external threats and internal challenges. Perhaps the end of the Cold War encouraged some citizens of the West to relax their guard, to take the future well-being of our political, economic and security systems for granted. Now, the "problem" for Western countries is dealing with a confluence of forces that challenge the "idea" of the West, its application in Western democracies and the international institutions founded on liberal internationalist principles.

The West of which we speak is defined by the values of liberal democracy, individual freedom, human rights, tolerance and equality under the rule of law. The West is an idea, or rather a basket of ideas. It is not defined by distinctions of race, culture, religion, language, nationalism, wealth or other traits that divide rather than unite human beings. It is not the West that President Trump has referred to as constituting "the bonds of culture, faith and tradition that make us who we are."[1] Trump's formulation threatens to close the door of the West to those of different cultures, faiths and traditions who, while differing in many ways, nonetheless accept and practice Western values.

This concept of the West has been shaped largely since the end of World War II. But the history is both much deeper and fraught with the challenges of change. This West traces its roots to the birthplace of democracy in Greece some 8,000 years ago. The period of Enlightenment – a movement among European intellectuals some 200 years ago – advanced the concept dramatically with its advocacy of relying on reason and rationalism rather than tradition, tribalism and religion to govern human relations. It celebrated science and the promotion of religious tolerance and governments based on constitutionalism with separation of church and state. This progress toward what we now call liberal internationalism nonetheless grew alongside the spread of slavery in Western states. Western governments initially used the concept to oppose the barbaric "East," or anything that was not European.

To understand the idea of the West today, it's important to recall that, even in recent historical periods, "the West" has not always represented the best that people can be, reminding ourselves that colonialism and robber barons were still features of Western civilization not many decades ago. Only after we acknowledge that history can we credibly argue that the West nonetheless developed some of the most powerful paradigms for human decency – individual liberty, human rights, and so on – and that the West can be defined as synonymous with these values. However, the struggle against ideas that run counter to these Western values continues, as demonstrated by recent political developments on both sides of the Atlantic. As one observer has noted, "The source of the West's evolutionary power has been its openness, its equality of rights, and its social trust."[2] All of those attributes have been called into question by the recent resurgence of illiberalism.

This, of course, is not the first time that such a threat has appeared. As author Thomas Ricks has recently observed, in the 1930s "The end of the Western way of life, and especially the death of liberal democracy, was a common theme in cultural life."[3] And we all know what came next.

The transatlantic traumas of 2016–17 have once again put

the West in jeopardy. The combination of external threats from Russia, disruptive radical Islamist terror and internal weaknesses in Western social, economic and political systems has formed a perfect storm. That storm endangers not only the security of Western democracies but also the values that have shaped the West since the end of World War II, and the institutions that operationalize them.

Then-US Secretary of State Dean Acheson told members of the Senate Foreign Relations Committee that the North Atlantic Treaty to which they were being asked to give their advice and consent "is far more than a defensive arrangement. It is an affirmation of the moral and spiritual values which we hold in common."[4] Nearly seventy years since the North Atlantic Treaty Organization (NATO) was founded and the beginning of the European community-building process, reaffirmation, reform and reactivation of these values will be required to preserve what we know as "the West."[5]

During the Cold War, it was generally accepted that Western nations included not only the transatlantic democracies but also several nations around the world that accepted, at least in principle, the North Atlantic Treaty's support for "democracy, individual liberty and the rule of law." The West therefore extends well beyond NATO and the European Union (EU), particularly as there are important partners in Asia and Australasia – Australia, New Zealand, Japan and South Korea in particular – that consider themselves part of this community of liberal democracies. These democracies may not become candidates for membership in NATO or the EU, but they will most likely continue to look to these organizations as critical components of the Western system. Russia will continue to see strengthening or enlarging membership of NATO and the EU as threatening to its interests, at least as currently defined in Moscow.

Ever since the signature of the North Atlantic Treaty in Washington on 4 April 1949, the United States, Canada and a constantly expanding number of European democracies have combined their resources to defend their security and democratic political systems against external threats. At the same time, many of the European democracies, urged on by the United States, developed the community system of integration that has produced today's European Union. NATO and the EU became the main institutional embodiments of the West. Most of the countries that considered themselves part of the West cooperated to defend it against communism, deter Soviet aggression, develop intense economic and financial ties across the Atlantic, and invited qualifying new democracies to join their ranks. They largely assumed that Western values would remain the touchstones for their political and economic development and the institutional arrangements intended to ensure their security and well-being.

On countless occasions over the past seventy years since the North Atlantic Treaty was signed, some observers have asserted that NATO is "only a military alliance." No doubt, NATO is a military alliance. But it is also true that, if it were only a military alliance, it would not be around well into the twenty-first century. As Wallace J. Thies has argued – albeit before Donald Trump became the definer of US policy toward the alliance – "Unlike many pre-1939 alliances, which collapsed at the first hint of troubles among the members, the democracies that make up the Atlantic Alliance have shown a willingness to do whatever it takes – even outright policy reversals – to heal a rift in the Alliance."[6] According to Thies, NATO is different from previous alliances in at least two key ways. First, it was established not just to meet a specific threat or serve a narrow purpose, but was designed to have much more lasting utility. Second, NATO was an alliance among liberal democracies with a value foundation that previous alliances had lacked – with strategic exceptions originally made for Portugal and for military juntas in Greece and Turkey on several occasions. Perhaps the big question now is whether that value foundation is still strong enough to resist some of the value-based threats that have emerged from within the alliance, as well as those that threaten from outside.

The values articulated in the preamble to the North Atlantic Treaty and their affirmation by US Secretary of State Acheson were not simply political rhetoric, designed to generate political support for a unique and demanding set of commitments. They defined the West.

In the late 1940s, leaders of NATO's founding states understood that a political philosophy – fascism – had not only led to Germany's power grab in Europe, but had also replaced democratic political systems across the continent. They also understood that the Soviet Union's World War II military role allied to the United States, as critical as it was to victory over Adolf Hitler's Nazi Germany, had positioned the Soviet Union to spread its power and ideology across the continent. The continental leaders – France in particular – wanted to ensure that Germany's power would never again be used to threaten French independence, and that democracy would remain safe from the fascist temptation that had just devastated Europe. The United States, joined by democratic forces in Western Europe, was concerned about the Soviet Union's post-war domination of Central and Eastern Europe and the threat that communist parties in Western Europe would lead to establishment of communist regimes there as well. That certainly seemed to be Soviet dictator Josef Stalin's objective.

So, even in the beginning, NATO had a political and economic as well as a military purpose. The goal was to stabilize Western Europe as insurance against a fascist or German revival, while resisting attempts by the Soviet Union to use democratic systems to take control of governments, as Moscow had done in the East, where governments in Poland, Czechoslovakia, Hungary, Romania, Bulgaria and the Eastern half of Germany were brought into the Soviet orbit.

NATO therefore was a military alliance whose purpose was to protect democratic, free market political and economic systems in the member states. The community-building process in Western Europe had been stimulated by the US Marshall Plan program of assistance to the war-torn European countries. The Marshall Plan had been offered to Central and Eastern European countries as well as to Western European ones, but the Soviet Union blocked them from participating. The United States placed a critically important condition on the recipients of

Marshall Plan aid: that they organize a cooperative effort to use the assistance most effectively. That cooperative effort provided the foundation for the community-building process that led to today's European Union. Irrespective of how one feels about the EU's current strengths and weaknesses, that process provided a Eurocentric partner to the Atlanticist NATO that stabilized Western Europe and protected democracy from potential internal and very real external threats. It is true that, during the Cold War, the values enumerated in the North Atlantic Treaty occasionally took second place when authoritarian regimes in NATO member nations were tolerated in the interest of maintaining a militarily strong alliance. But NATO's survival beyond the end of the Cold War suggested that its value foundation and the inherent logic of Euro-Atlantic cooperation remained important ingredients in the glue that was holding the alliance together.

In 1989, a process began in which the benign tides of history seemed to be washing away the military rationale for NATO. On 9–10 November 1989, East and West Berliners breached the Berlin Wall that communist authorities had erected in 1961 to prevent East Germans from fleeing to West Germany. This became the first step toward reunification of East and West Germany. On 3 October 1990, the Federal Republic of Germany absorbed the German Democratic Republic, creating a unified Germany. NATO's North Atlantic Council welcomed the unified country as a full member of NATO. Like autumn leaves, communist regimes started falling throughout Eastern Europe, with the Soviet leadership unwilling or unable to stop the unraveling of their alliance and, ultimately, of the Soviet Union itself.

The revolutionary changes in Europe at the end of the Cold War left the transatlantic allies with historic choices about how to organize European security. NATO had been the West's indispensable institution during the Cold War. But at the end of the Cold War many wondered whether the alliance would or should be swept away by the accelerating winds of change. The NATO members had already been working hard to improve security relations in Europe, largely through negotiating arms control and confidence-building measures with the Soviet Union and its

Warsaw Pact allies. As 1990 opened, the authoritarian regimes that had held the Warsaw Pact together were crumbling, and the Warsaw Pact itself was not far behind. The West Germans and the post-communist East German authorities began negotiating reunification under the watchful eyes of the Soviet Union, the United States, France and the United Kingdom.

In this heady atmosphere, many thoughtful analysts and officials on both sides of the Atlantic questioned what NATO's place might be in a world in which the Warsaw Pact had been disbanded and the Soviet Union was withdrawing its forces from Central Europe. On the other hand, new leaders of former Warsaw Pact nations were already focusing on the goal of joining NATO, followed closely by membership in the EU.

Early in 1990, very few Western observers were willing to talk about NATO opening its membership to former Warsaw Pact states. In fact, a variety of quite different concepts for the future organization of European security competed for official and public approval. Some observers argued it might be best to keep the Warsaw Pact in business to help organize future security in Europe. Others suggested that NATO had outlived its usefulness because there was no longer any threat. Such advocates believed that the Conference on Security and Cooperation in Europe, to which all European states, the United States and Canada belonged, could take over responsibility for maintaining peace and security on the Continent. Some Europeans, including French president François Mitterrand and British prime minister Margaret Thatcher, preferred alternatives to German reunification while the United States facilitated accomplishment of West Germany's long-term goal.

As the world seemed to be changing all around them, the leaders of NATO countries decided that they should address the question of whether NATO was needed. Instinctively, the governments of all member states, as well as NATO Secretary General Manfred Woerner, believed that NATO should be preserved – even if they were not fully agreed as to why. Some officials argued that NATO was more than a military alliance and was based, in fact, on a community of values that rose above any specific military threat. Others maintained that the Soviet Union remained an alien society that could produce new threats in the future. They saw NATO as an "insurance policy" against a future fire in the European house. Some pointed to new risks and uncertainties that could best be dealt with through NATO's approach, in which like-minded countries work together to handle security problems.

The key factor, illustrating that the member states still considered NATO more than "just a military alliance," was the reaction of allies to the desire of former Warsaw Pact states and even former Soviet republics to join the alliance. Their primary motivation was universally to gain protection against ever again being dominated by their neighbor to the East. But the allies decided that the aspiring members would have to align not only with NATO's defense provisions, but also with its political guidelines. The NATO enlargement study of 1995 specified that new members would have to be contributors to security, not just consumers. It provided a path toward compatibility with NATO's military structures. But more importantly, it suggested that aspirants must establish civilian control over their militaries as well as functioning democratic systems based on the rule of law, guaranteeing individual liberties and facilitating free market economies.

If the North Atlantic Treaty provided the broad outline for what it means to be a member of the West, and I think it does, the NATO enlargement study provided the roadmap to membership in that club. When the same countries also sought to join the EU, they faced a similar set of value requirements, as well as a very demanding set of economic, financial, social, administrative and political conditions. The combination of the NATO and EU membership processes set prospective new members on a very clear course. But it did not guarantee that all new members of either or both organizations would always stay true to that course.

Some developments in recent years suggest that both the EU and NATO should worry about the quality of the democracies of those which have already made it in, not just those which want in. That question is discussed later. But for now, we turn to the external threats to the West that dismissed any Pollyannaish dreams of a conflict-free future. We then look at the internal weaknesses of the West suggested by the gains of illiberal political parties in Europe, Turkey's dramatic movement away from its Western moorings, the UK's departure from the EU and the election of Donald Trump in the United States, all of which make the West much more vulnerable to the external threats discussed next.

Notes

1   The White House, "Remarks by President Trump to the people of Poland | July 6, 2017," www.whitehouse.gov/the-press-office/2017/07/06/remarks-president-trump-people-poland-july-6-2017 [accessed 6 October 2017].

2   Bill Emmott, *The Fate of the West* (New York: Public Affairs, 2017), 7.

3   Thomas E. Ricks, *Churchill & Orwell: The Fight for Freedom* (New York: Penguin, 2017), 45.

4   US Senate Committee on Foreign Relations, North Atlantic Treaty, Hearings before the Committee on Foreign Relations, 81st Cong., 1st sess., 27–29 April and 2–3 May 1949.

5   For a more detailed interpretation of this history, on which this chapter draws, see Stanley R. Sloan, *Defense of the West: NATO, the European Union and the Transatlantic Bargain* (Manchester: Manchester University Press, 2016).

6   Wallace J. Thies, *Why NATO Endures* (New York: Cambridge University Press, 2009), 307.

2

Islamist and Russian threats challenging the West

> As President I wanted to share with Russia ... which I have the right to do, facts pertaining to terrorism and airline safety ... plus I want Russia to greatly step up their fight against ISIS & terrorism."[1]
>
> Donald J. Trump, after sharing highly classified intelligence with the Russian Foreign Minister and Moscow's Ambassador to the United States

How can we see Islamist terror and Russian aggression as companion threats to the West when terrorists target Russia as well as the United States and its allies? Isn't this why President Trump has argued for cooperating with Russia against Islamist terrorism? Good questions. There are answers.

The threats posed by Islamist terror and Russian aggression present themselves in very different ways. But they have one thing in common: both seek to create political and economic chaos in the West, undermining Western economic, political and security systems and, in extremis, creating a new world order in which the West is not the dominant player. They are by no means the only authoritarian regimes out there, but they are the two that most actively seek to undermine the Western system and its values. In the time of transatlantic traumas, both threats have worked diligently and with some success. They have, to some degree, already changed the normal way of life in Western countries, ranging from the much more pervasive security measures encountered almost everywhere, to dealing with the overwhelming flow of refugees from the war-torn Middle

East, to the destabilizing British plan to leave the EU, and to the election of Donald Trump as a disruptive American president.

From the Taliban regime in Afghanistan blowing up historic artifacts there to the Islamic State of Iraq and the Levant (known variously as "ISIL," "ISIS," or "Daesh")[2] destroying precious symbols of Middle Eastern ancient history, the radical Islamists seek to wipe out any vestiges other than those that are part of their perceived pre-history. At the same time, they seek to establish a "caliphate," or kingdom, ruled by an interpretation of Sharia law that replaces values and institutions of the West. They reach out with terrorism against Western states to destabilize Western systems and demoralize Western populations.

As for Russia, even though Moscow has been tormented by Islamist terror, primarily from separatists in Russia's Chechnya republic, it shares the goal of disrupting the West. Russian president Putin's strategy seeks to replace Western systems with those that give Russia a more prominent role and are consistent with its authoritarian style of government.

How did these threats develop in recent years, and what is their present status?

Islamist terrorist threat: why do they hate us?

Why do they hate us? This question is on the minds of many in the West. The answer is not a simple one, nor is there one answer that is endorsed by all experts on Islamist terror.

The answer, some say, is in quite recent history. When the United States and its allies ousted Saddam Hussein and his Sunni-dominated regime from power, it created a leadership void quickly filled by Iraqi Shia Muslims, who had long been repressed by the Sunni minority. Under the government led by Iraqi Nouri al-Maliki, installed with US protection after the ousting of Hussein, the remnants of Hussein's regime essentially provided the motivation and foot soldiers for what became the Islamic State. This certainly is part of the answer, but it most likely is too simple. The next step back in history leads to al

Qaeda, and its leader, the late Osama bin Laden, who master-minded the 9/11 attacks on the United States from his base in Afghanistan. The Islamic Afghan Taliban regime hosted and protected bin Laden and his followers. Following the attacks, the United States and its Western allies went to war against the Taliban regime, ousted it, and then destroyed al Qaeda's infrastructure in the country and eventually killed bin Laden at his hideout in Abbottabad, Pakistan. Ousted from Afghanistan, al Qaeda, led by subordinates to bin Laden, re-established itself in north Africa, where it continued its mission of attacking the West as well as moderate Muslim regimes and political forces. But ISIL was by that time becoming the prime mover for radical Islamists in the war against the West, drawing strength from disenfranchised Iraqi Sunnis and from an offshoot of the Iraqi al Qaeda branch that had managed to garner support from other smaller groups in the region.

As experts on the Middle East well know, the history of this problem is much deeper. Some would find the explanation of today's Islamist terrorist threat in the US involvement in the Middle East since the end of World War II. Others would go back further, placing much of the onus on the European powers that dominated and divided lands according to colonialist and profit motivations rather than local logic or considerations for the native populations, leaving behind a deep resentment of Western values, interests and intrusions.

While it is tempting to attribute the entirety of Islamist ter-rorism to various Western transgressions, it seems clear that Islam also has some internal problems of its own. Islamist terror has taken many more lives of other Muslims than it has of Americans and Europeans. And we know that Muslims around the world oppose and fight terrorism manifested by a small minority of those following Islam, just as most Christians con-demn individuals in their ranks, including some anti-abortion activists and white supremacists, who use terrorist tactics on behalf of their Christian beliefs. There is a need for discussion and debate among those of the Islamic faith about the legitimate goals of their religion, its relationship to modernity, relationship to other religions, and compatibility with Western values of individual liberty, democracy and the rule of law. Dr. Janet Breslin-Smith argues that dealing with Islamist terrorism will eventually require such a discussion among Muslims. She writes that Muslims must ask and answer several questions:

- *Is Islam a religion of tolerance, or not? If the faithful believe it to be the final revelation of God, how can they find a way to accept those of other faiths, or no faith?*
- *Does Islam embrace equality, compassion, and justice? What does its Holy book, the Quran say about corruption, injustice and materialism?*
- *If ISIS and such groups have "hijacked" Islam, what are the faithful going to do about it?*[3]

Islam's internal divisions

For many of those who are not Muslim, perhaps the most puzzling thing about Islam is its internal divisions. The most important one is between those who follow the Sunni branch of Islam – some 85 percent of all Muslims – and those who adhere to the Shia side. The division between Shia and Sunni, the two major Islamic sects, stems from disagreement over Muhammad's rightful successor. Shia believe Ali, the Prophet's relative by marriage, was named successor and that Ali's descendants are the rightful *Imams*, or leaders. Within Shi'ism there are factions who follow disparate lines of succession, but the unifying link is the belief in a hereditary pattern of rightful leadership of the *umma*, or Muslim community.

Sunni belief does not include hereditary caliph succession; rather, Sunnis believe that Allah legitimizes a *caliph* (leader) based on his piety and implementation of a wise interpretation of *Shari'a* (God's will for human life). The Sunni faith places more focus on structure: a structured caliphate, structured schools of jurisprudence and structured legal systems.

This sectarian division over the interpretation of original Islamic text and history has contributed to several modern conflicts and threatened the security of the global system. A history of Shia marginalization by Sunni factions means that when Shia groups gain power, such as in Iran after the 1979 revolution, Sunni fundamentalists, notably Wahhabis, often arise in opposition. Sectarian Shia/Sunni conflicts have contributed to the war in Iraq, the Arab Spring, the Syrian civil war, the Yemeni civil war and ISIL's push for a global caliphate, all of which have affected not only the countries in question but their neighbors and allies. ISIL, one of the current greatest threats to international peace and security, is a Sunni organization explicitly dedicated to dismantling both Shia and Western power through military action, horrific terror attacks and brutality. ISIL's aggressions have created floods of refugees, leading to economic and social struggles throughout the Middle East, Africa and Europe.

Middle Eastern turmoil and refugees

Despite the many attempts by the United States and other Western powers to promote peace and stability in the Middle East, turmoil has continued to spiral out of control – turmoil to which the West contributed. Although there remains no peace in sight between Israel and the Palestinians, the focus has shifted away from this formerly leading touchstone of Middle Eastern conflict to the new threat posed by ISIL, whose prominence grew dramatically when it mounted a major terrorist assault on Paris in November 2015. Meanwhile, the much hoped for democratic reform of the region growing out of the Arab Spring moved steadily toward a chaotic Middle Eastern Winter.

One of the immediate threats posed by ISIL's expansion in the region was to add to the refugee crisis in the Mediterranean, as citizens of war-torn countries across the Middle East and North Africa sought to escape the fighting, as well as fleeing Assad's brutal dictatorship in Syria, seeking safer homes and opportunities in Europe. Hundreds of refugees were dying daily, as they crowded onto less than seaworthy vessels, having paid exorbitant fees to profiteering "entrepreneurs" who mostly abandoned them once afloat. The exodus continues, as do the accompanying tragedies, although the anti-ISIL coalition has been eliminating the group's territorial grip in Iraq and Syria.

NATO and EU responses

The burden of dealing with this surge of asylum seekers fell first on the EU and NATO states along the northern rim of the Mediterranean, particularly Italy, Greece and Turkey. But as the numbers escalated, and Italy threatened to "share" the refugees with other EU states, the EU recognized that it would have to take steps not only in response to the humanitarian aspects of the crisis but also with the threats to Europe's open border policies. On 23 April 2015, the EU Council issued a statement finding that "The situation in the Mediterranean is a tragedy."[4] The EU members pledged to strengthen their presence in the Mediterranean to try to prevent further loss of life and to work with other countries to deal with the root causes of the emergency.

The refugee crisis emerged partially because ISIL had taken control of substantial parts of Iraq and was spreading into adjoining states. Although President Obama, at the September 2014 NATO Summit in Wales, managed to get a strong NATO consensus behind US policy to "degrade and destroy" ISIL, the actual fighting fell outside NATO's mandate. It was a somewhat unusual case of the allies publishing a strong NATO statement against a threat without supporting collective action, under a NATO flag, to deal with it.

ISIL's growth and influence can be partially attributed to its hugely successful propaganda machine. Its promises of community and prosperity under the caliphate appealed to disenfranchised and alienated populations. Its effective use of social media ensured that messages were spread quickly and far. In 2016, it was estimated that approximately 5,000 Europeans traveled to Syria and Iraq to train as Islamist fighters or recruiters.

After ISIL's "caliphate" started losing control of territory in Syria and Iraq, European volunteers were told to return to Europe and carry out simple, "lone wolf"-style attacks to increase an atmosphere of fear. These ISIL supporters were also encouraged to recruit as many as possible in their countries. While ISIL terror attacks have been concentrated in the Middle East and Europe, fear of ISIL and Islamist terror in general has spread across the Atlantic to the United States.

For the United States, ISIL represented a serious threat to the accomplishments of US forces and policies in Iraq. Some NATO allies, particularly the United Kingdom, shared that concern. But there was a bigger picture: ISIL not only represented a source of dramatic instability in the Middle East and North Africa, but was also a direct challenge to the values and interests on which membership in both NATO and the EU was founded. Moreover, ISIL spokesmen promised that, from their growing base of operations, they would carry their threat to those values and interests through terrorist attacks on the United States and Canada as well as on next-door Europe.

Islamist and Russian threats converge in Syria

In September 2015, the threats posed by Russia and ISIL converged in a somewhat unexpected manner, raising some difficult questions for the West. Russia deployed fighter bombers and troops to Syria to support the regime of President Bashar al-Assad, which had been losing ground both to ISIL and a loose mix of other anti-regime forces, some supported by the United States. Syria had remained a key ally for Russia at the end of the Cold War, having been an important Middle Eastern ally for the Soviet Union since 1956, including the provision of a key naval base in Tartus on the Mediterranean. Russia described its military support for Assad as intended to fight ISIL, but the missions of the deployed Russian forces made it clear that Russia was targeting Western-supported anti-Assad forces equally if not more than ISIL. The challenge for the United States and its allies was how to continue supporting "moderate" opponents of Assad and encouraging Russia to train its guns on ISIL while not coming into accidental conflict with Russian forces.

The Russian threat

When the Cold War ended, Russia descended into chaos, featuring an ill-fated attempt at democracy accompanied by a wild-west financial and economic environment in which Russian oligarchs seized "get rich quick" opportunities. Eventually, with many Russians yearning for the stability that they had known in Soviet times, Vladimir Putin offered that prospect. Putin, a former KGB officer who moved from a political position in St. Petersburg to become an advisor to President Yeltsin, then head of the FSB, a post-Soviet successor to the KGB, and then prime minister, began reasserting centralized political power in Moscow. He reacted strongly to the fact that NATO had opened its membership to former Warsaw Pact states and even Soviet republics when those states pleaded for protection from future Russian domination. He portrayed the process as anti-Russian – which in some respects it was – and used NATO and the United States as external threats to help justify his increasingly autocratic internal control.

As tensions with the West deepened over Russia's seizure of the Crimea and military intervention in Ukraine, it became clear that President Putin was contesting the entire Western-oriented system of security in Europe and globally that, from his point of view, gave Russia's interests short shrift. Putin knew that NATO, given its reliance on consensus decision-making, was not an offensive threat against Russia and likely would never be one. But Putin did see a threat: the danger that Western political and economic systems, becoming more and more popular around Russia's borders, would ultimately infect Russia itself, bringing Putin's form of autocratic rule into question. Putin argues that he is simply reacting to encirclement by the West, and he undoubtedly sees Western-style democracy as a threat, while using the image of a NATO military threat as a rationale for internal domestic control and external intervention.

Following the decades-long Cold War, pitting the communist Soviet Union against the democratic/capitalist West, a newly chaotic Russian Federation emerged in the 1990s, led, but not tamed, by President Boris Yeltsin. This turmoil created the political conditions for Yeltsin's ambitious deputy chief of presidential staff Vladimir Putin's Machiavellian rise to power. He was appointed acting president at the turn of the century and has virtually maintained power ever since. Putin has created what Marvin Kalb calls a "kleptomaniacal autocracy": a system in which the rule of law is subordinated to Putin's despotic will.[5] Under Putin's rule, overt autocracy reigns supreme in modern-day Russia.

It would be one thing if Putin's anti-Westernism affected only internal Russian life, but his agenda and actions stretch far beyond Russia's borders. Putin's autocracy seeks to undermine the very foundations of the West: economic and political institutions, alliances and what Putin sees as a Western-dominated world order. During his first term, Putin supported Russia's joining of the World Trade Organization. But that stance would be unthinkable today, both in terms of Putin's priorities and Western sanctions imposed after the seizure of Crimea. His developing anti-Westernism assaults core liberal democratic beliefs – which, in a larger sense, form the basis of what we consider the West. Evaluating Putin's beliefs and prejudices is critical because he will most likely continue to challenge Western ideology so long as he holds power.

If Putin has "one foot in the old ways of doing business," as former US President Barack Obama alleged,[6] then Putin's obsessive control over media coverage best exemplifies his propagandistic tendencies. Before his first year as president was over, Putin had established control of the three main Russian television networks. Under the Kremlin's watchful eye, mass media is manipulated; the few independent channels that remain project a vague, damaged pluralism. In practice, journalists avoid topics known to be sensitive to the Kremlin. The pressure is not always subtle. The assassination of journalist and Putin critic Anna Politkovskaya was an explicit warning to Russian journalists. President Putin, much like President Trump, regards the media as the "opposition." While Putin and Trump share an aversion to critical press, Putin has been far more successful in silencing his media critics. Whereas the American system includes strong checks on executive power, Putin's Russia depends on authoritarian control rather than rule of law. Putin's condemnation of free media and human rights – among other core Western beliefs – reveals an authoritarianism that denies many democratic freedoms taken for granted in the West.

Putin is a strong social conservative, demonstrated by the limits he has placed on a wide variety of human rights and his particularly violent crackdown on homosexuality. Those who protest Putin's rule, like the women of the Russian punk rock group Pussy Riot, become targets of ridicule, violence, arrest and imprisonment. In this area, Putin has closely aligned with the Russian Orthodox Church, which has in return offered strong support and endorsement of Putin's socially conservative policies. Putin's conversion from a servant of "godless" communism in the Soviet Union to near-sainthood status in the Russian Orthodox Church of the Russian Federation has been just short of miraculous.

The way that Putin punishes dissidents – or, in some cases, makes them disappear – reveals a twisted web of human rights abuses and unchecked presidential power. The already long list of persecuted dissidents includes Mikhail Khodorkovsky, Aleksandr Litvinenko, Anna Politkovskaya and Aleksandr Perepilichnyy. Leading political critic Boris Nemtsov was killed in February 2015, ostensibly by Chechen assassins, but many saw Putin's hand behind the hit. More recently, authorities in the summer of 2017 locked up Aleksei Navalny, Putin's leading challenger in the 2018 presidential election, for twenty-five days, illustrating Putin's unabashed meddling in the election process. The 2018 election results could allow Putin not only to retain power but to expand further his already quite comprehensive authoritarian rule.

Impact of the Russian threat

Tensions between Putin's Russia and the West came to a head in 2014 when Russian special forces – the infamous Little Green Men – were inserted surreptitiously and took control of Ukraine's Crimea region. Russian annexation of the Crimea, which followed by a few years virtual annexation of two of Georgia's regions, was a gross violation of the Budapest Memorandum, a 1994 agreement in which Russia, the United States and the United Kingdom agreed that, in exchange for recognition of its borders by all parties, Ukraine would give up the residual nuclear forces left over from their deployment there during the Soviet period.

At the same time, pro-Russian separatist forces were establishing themselves in the Ukrainian regions of Donetsk and Luhansk, apparently with covert support from Moscow. These two regions had consistently stood against Ukrainian membership in NATO and preferred closer ties to neighboring Russia than to the European Union, which the new "Maidan" government in Kiev was seeking.

"Some Western politicians," Putin claimed in a March 2014 public speech, "hope to put us in a deteriorating social and economic situation."[7] He portrayed Ukrainian desires to join NATO and the EU as threats to Russia. Ukraine's signature of an association agreement with the EU in 2014 increased tensions between Europe and Russia. Tensions increased further when the Russian-supported separatists used a Russian missile system to shoot down Malaysian Flight 17 over Ukrainian territory, with 298 on board, including many Dutch citizens. The Russian government dismissed the conclusions of a Dutch-led investigation of the attack on MH17, calling the allegations "politically motivated."[8]

As demonstrated by the MH17 tragedy, Russian aggression affects more than Crimean Tatars and Ukrainian Donbass residents. Russian aggression led Western powers to boot Russia out of the G8 economic grouping, making it the "G7"; impose economic sanctions on Russia; and lead a hundred nations of the UN General Assembly to judge as invalid the Russian-manipulated Crimea referendum that supposedly showed popular Crimean support for the annexation.

Putin was emboldened by his apparent belief that the West was corruptible, failing and weak-willed. His nationalist foreign policy was based on the judgment that a weak West would make for a stronger, more influential Russia. Putin scoffed at the 1976 Helsinki Accords' long-established agreement not to change borders by force, to which Moscow had previously agreed. And Putin has done a good sales job at home. A 2014 poll conducted by the Russia Public Opinion Center found that over 80 percent of Russians supported Putin's use of force on behalf of Russian nationalism and believed that Crimea should remain a part of Russia.[9]

As tensions with the West deepened over Russia's seizure of Crimea and military intervention in Ukraine, it became clear that President Putin was contesting the entire system of security in Europe and globally based on Western interests. From his — and many Russians' — point of view, the annexation of Crimea was justified by the need to protect ethnic Russians abroad, an ethnic-historical minority found prominently in Ukraine, Belarus and the Baltic States. The annexation of Crimea most poignantly proved the danger of bringing such ideology to life. The Russian–Ukrainian conflict put a face to the name of Putinism. Operating under the vague promise to protect ethnic Russians abroad, Putin could easily push the envelope even further than Crimea.

Putin's attack on Western democracy

Putin's most telling response to Western economic sanctions and pledges of increased NATO defense efforts was not strictly in the military realm, even though the Russian military did step up harassment of Western air and naval units operating near Russia and probed Western defenses around the world. The most worrisome Russian strategy, however, was to attack

Western democracy at its heart: the process of democratic election of Western governments.

The meddling began in Europe, where Moscow sent overt as well as clandestine assistance to far-right illiberal political groups and parties. For example, the French National Front reportedly received a 9.4 million Euro loan from Russia in November 2014. Press sources at the time reported that Marine Le Pen, the party's leader, admired Putin as a "strong" leader. As France approached presidential elections in 2017, Le Pen emerged as a leading contender for the presidency and brazenly traveled to Moscow to meet with her ideological soulmate. The Russian intervention did not produce a Le Pen victory, but there was no indication that Putin would suspend such interference in French or other elections in the future.

The most alarming intervention came when Putin ordered his intelligence agencies and their various assets to intervene in the 2016 American presidential election on behalf of Republican nominee Donald Trump. Although the US Obama administration became aware of the active measures, it was only after Trump had won the presidency that reports emerged from the US intelligence community that Russia had not only intervened by hacking into computer systems of the Democratic National Committee, but had also encouraged or directed Wikileaks to release information to try to undermine Democratic nominee Hillary Clinton's candidacy. In the first months of Trump's presidency, the FBI as well as numerous congressional committees intensified investigations into whether Trump or his associates had colluded with the Russians and whether they had then tried to impede the investigations of possible collusion.

No matter how the various investigations turn out, Putin's Russia clearly managed to disrupt both the American electoral process and to cast a dark cloud over the Trump presidency. Trump himself, of course, darkened the cloud considerably with his refusal to accept that Moscow was behind the tampering and should be punished for it.

It also seems clear that Russia, particularly given its success in the United States, will continue to try to influence Western elections to encourage the election of politicians that Moscow thinks will favor Russian interests as well as to demonstrate weaknesses in Western democracies.

The convergence of Islamist terrorist and Russian threats

There are, of course, other threats to Western interests. The unpredictable behavior of North Korea and its progress toward intercontinental nuclear striking capabilities is an urgent challenge to American security. Conflict in the Middle East and Afghanistan is part of the terrorist threat posed by radical Islamist movements like ISIL. Continuing turbulence in the Middle Eastern and South/Central Asia poses a wide variety of threats to the United States and its allies. And China's growing power will pose additional challenges.

But the convergence of Islamist radical attempts and Russian strategic objectives, both aimed at undermining the West and its political/economic/security systems, is the most worrisome political threat to the West. The fact that both threats have found their way directly into Western political systems and daily lives makes it doubly damaging. ISIL recruits young Europeans and Americans, trains them in the Middle East and then sends them back home to conduct terrorist attacks, or indoctrinates them in place through social media. For the time being, Russia uses targeted killings mainly against domestic opponents of Putin, and has used blunt force against former Soviet Republics Ukraine and Georgia to punish them for wanting to follow a Western democratic path into their future. Russian attacks on Western democracies are more sophisticated and complex than ISIL's frontal terrorist approach. But they are just as, if not more, effective and dangerous.

In Chapter 3, we move on to discuss how and why developments inside Western countries have created fertile ground for the growth of populist movements, perhaps combining with external threats to create the potential for a "perfect storm," calling the Western liberal democratic system into question.

Notes

1   Donald J. Trump, "As President I wanted to share with Russia...,"
     Twitter, 16 May 2017, https://twitter.com/realDonaldTrump/sta
     tus/864436162567471104?ref_src=twsrc%5Etfw&ref_url=http%
     3A%2F%2Fwww.cnn.com%2F2017%2F05%2F16%2Fpolitics%
     2Fdonald-trump-russia-right%2Findnex.html; and https://twit
     ter.com/realDonaldTrump/status/864438529472049152?ref_
     src=twsrc%5Etfw&ref_url=http%3A%2F%2Fwww.cnn.com%
     2F2017%2F05%2F16%2Fpolitics%2Fdonald-trump-russia-rig
     ht%2Findex.html [accessed 1 November 2017].

2   "Daesh" is used by some, including the French, as a term with
     derogatory implications because it sounds like the Arabic word
     for "sowers of discord." For the sake of simplicity, this book
     uses "ISIL" when referring to the Islamic State.

3   Janet Breslin-Smith, "What Obama may find in Arabia next
     week: a sense of authority in crisis," *Foreign Policy*, 11 April 2016.

4   European Council, "Special meeting of the European Council,
     23 April 2015 – statement," www.consilium.europa.eu/en/
     press/press-releases/2015/04/23-special-euco-statement/ [acc
     essed 6 October 2017].

5   Marvin Kalb, *Imperial Gamble: Putin, Ukraine, and the New Cold
     War* (Washington, DC: Brookings, 2015).

6   Chris McGreal, "Barack Obama: Putin has one foot in the past,"
     The Guardian, 2 July 2009, www.theguardian.com/world/2009/
     jul/02/obama-putin-us-russia-relations [accessed 6 October
     2017].

7   Steven Lee Myers and Ellen Barry, "Putin reclaims Crimea for
     Russia and bitterly denounces the West," *New York Times*, 18
     March 2014, www.nytimes.com/2014/03/19/world/europe/
     ukraine.html?_r=0 [accessed 6 October 2017].

8   Roland Oliphant and Senay Boztas, "MH17 investigation:
     Moscow denounces 'biased' investigation as prosecutors
     say missile came from Russia," *The Telegraph*, 28 September
     2016, www.telegraph.co.uk/news/2016/09/28/mh17-investiga
     tion-prosecutors-to-reveal-where-missile-that-down/ [accessed
     2 November 2017].

9   Russian Public Research Center, "Crimea in Russia: restoration
     of historical justice," Press Release No. 1621, 24 March 2014,
     https://wciom.com/index.php?id=61&uid=937   [accessed   3
     November 2017].

3

Malaise in the West

> Populists claim that they, and they alone, represent the people.
>
> Jan-Werner Müller, *What is populism?*[1]

While the Russian and Islamist threats to the West confronted Western nations with a diverse set of problems, storms were brewing on several home fronts as well. A surge in what has been called "populism" gave new life to a variety of right-wing political parties or candidates playing on otherwise legitimate popular fears and concerns, advocating simplistic, sloganeering political approaches that challenge the assumptions of established Western liberal democracy. Such politicians and parties have thrown around their political weight in several countries, exercising power in some, including the United States, Hungary, Poland, Switzerland and Turkey.

Sources of discontent

There is no single explanation for the rising popularity of illiberalism, but a combination of factors has produced a general sense of malaise. The Great Recession, starting in 2008, left millions of Americans and Europeans without jobs and in debt. While the job market has recovered, real wages have not, and a significant portion of European and American electorates believe that the system and its leaders have let them down. This certainly describes many supporters of Donald Trump and of far-right politicians in Europe as well. Another factor is concern that refugees, driven from their homes by conflicts in the Middle East and elsewhere, will not only bring terrorist threats home to Western states but will also threaten economic well-being, particularly among those who are already suffering the most from unemployment and other residual impacts of the Great Recession.

There is also a perception that the process of European integration, expanding international trade and globalism are undermining the way of life of average citizens. This perception is further aggravated by the fact that the share of wealth in Western democracies held by the famous "1 percent" continues to grow. Governance appears to be moving further and further away from local and individual control, whether due to EU regulations in Europe or Washington bureaucracy in the United States. Finally, the pace of life and development of technology have moved faster than the ability of many citizens to adjust to or even comprehend, making more people feel disenfranchised and disadvantaged.

On both sides of the Atlantic, every new terrorist attack provides fertile ground for fear-mongering politicians. In this area, the terrorists and the illiberal politicians both benefit from terrorist attacks that have a huge impact on the public's sense of safety but that have little chance on their own of bringing governments to their knees.

As a result, extremist political movements throughout Europe, and in the United States, found greater public resonance for their attacks on Western unity, and even the validity of a Western identity. These troubling internal divisions – inside and among Western states – could combine with the external threats to form a "perfect storm." That storm could blow away transatlantic unity and, with it, the definition and reality of "the West."

Many of these parties share worrying commonalities, including:

- opposing their countries' memberships in the European Union and NATO;
- favoring more autocratic forms of government; and
- sympathizing with Russian President Vladimir Putin's perspectives on politics, culture, religion and strategic issues.

We know that populism and nationalism have played major roles in the growth of support for extreme rightist parties. Neither populism nor nationalism is inherently inconsistent with democracy. But extremist politicians and would-be leaders use populist and nationalist appeals to play on fears, base instincts, racism, religious bias and historical grievances to generate support for their agendas. Those agendas often include personal power and wealth for the politicians who seek to turn popular fears and nationalistic sentiments into something ugly, and undemocratic. Some illiberal leaders emerged as part of the general discontent with liberal democracy and economy, but others were established politicians who seized on the circumstances to improve their political prospects.

Trumpism

It seems clear that the economic factors discussed above play a role in stimulating such tendencies, but other factors contribute as well. Just prior to Donald Trump's election as American president, *New York Times* editorial writer, Roger Cohen, asked how is it possible that Trump could become American president? He answered his own question with a list of factors, many of which have their counterparts in European countries. They include fear of terrorism, amplified by modern technology, two wars in which the United States has not found victory, consequences of the Great Recession for the middle class while the top 1 percent get even richer, concern about job loss, and finally "because Trump speaks to the basest but also some of the most ineradicable traits of human beings – their capacity for mob anger, their racist resentments, their cruelty, their lust, their search for scapegoats, their insecurities – and promises a miraculous makeover."[2] Cohen is right. History, including the American experience, is filled with examples of these negative qualities. They are all too common in today's politics.

As we know, the 2016 elections in the United States left the country with a president who did not win a majority of the popular vote (trailing Hillary Clinton by almost 3 million votes), but whose electoral base mostly held together for a while despite the administration's troubled early months. The solidity of this core of support can be explained in part by Donald Trump's effective appeal to Americans who were unhappy with their economic circumstances. Many Americans who had lost their jobs during the Great Recession felt that they had been left behind in the recovery. Even when the job market improved, wages did not. Some argue that Trump's victory was partly the product of the Democratic Party giving "cultural politics preference over real politics," which the late Stanford philosopher Richard Rorty in 1998 had predicted could split the traditional Democratic coalition between the middle and working classes.[3]

Trump's rhetoric built on criticism of the eight years of Barack Obama's presidency during which the Republican Party had largely refused cooperation with the president and promised to undo his policies, including his healthcare program, if they captured the White House. Another major factor was his focus on what he called "radical Islamic terror," a term that many saw as blaming all of Islam for a phenomenon that was condemned by the vast majority of Muslims. He argued that America's too-permissive approach to illegal, and even legal, immigration had not only been costly to the country's financial well-being but also increased the risk of terrorists slipping in to attack Americans. These positions were then translated into attempts by the Trump administration to limit travel from largely-Muslim countries to the United States and proposals to build a wall along the US border with Mexico. This focus on immigration as part of Trump's appeal to his base brought him into line with the radical right populist movements and parties in Europe.

In August 2017, Trump's reliance on support from some of

the most dangerous elements of his base apparently influenced his decision not to put the blame for violent and deadly clashes in Charlottesville, Virginia specifically where it belonged – on white supremacists, members of the KKK and neo-fascists, leading enemies of the American liberal democratic tradition. David Duke, former leader of the KKK, bragged that the far-right groups were supporting Trump's objectives and said Trump should remember that it was "white Americans" who put him in office. After Trump failed specifically to criticize the far-right groups, and intentionally suggest that "all sides" were to blame, the *Washington Post* reported that a neo-Nazi and white supremacy website, *The Daily Stormer*, attacked the many Republicans who had denounced white supremacists and the president's vague response to their violence. The website said it liked his response, saying "Trump comments were good. He didn't attack us... Really, really good. God bless him."[4] The incident suggested that the extreme right in the United States, although a small minority in the US population, remains an important and divisive factor in American politics, particularly so long as it is coddled by the president.

Refugees as an issue

A cornerstone of the emerging populist politicians' rhetoric is the idea of speaking for "the people" and defending a certain set of rights and values from others. Whether those "others" are a country's elites, or minority groups based on class, race, sexuality, religious creed or ethnicity, this populism is based on creating a small community by alienating many others. Across Europe, migrants and refugees are the frequent targets of such alienation or discrimination. Populist leaders conflate migration with increased terrorism, attempting to prove that the West's generosity toward refugees puts at risk the safety of its citizens, even though most European terror attacks since 2015 have been committed by European nationals. In an age of "alternative facts" where truth can be elusive, so long as populist right-wing politicians find a suitable scapegoat for multiple aspects of a country's economic and social struggles, a surprisingly large number of people will accept their explanations. Of course, when faced with frequent, devastating terror attacks and a sudden influx of people with vastly differing cultures, religion, and values, some Europeans (and Americans thanks to Trump's anti-immigrant stance) perceive a connection between immigration and terrorism, regardless of facts. Add in fears about unemployment and job-stealing already exacerbated by visa-free work permits throughout the EU, and you have an effective combination of us-vs-them, anti-migration sentiment.

The European populist radical right

Populist radical right (PRR) parties in continental Europe have come to represent a formidable challenge to the liberal transatlantic order. One expert has defined populism as a political tactic that assumes that "good people" are betrayed by an "evil elite."[5] Ironically, populist parties may be led by the very elites they decry, as is suggested by Donald Trump's populist following in the United States. The specific brand of populism that has risen in Europe has been called the "populist radical right" by Dutch political scientist Cas Mudde, and that term has largely been accepted by his colleagues in the field.[6]

PRRs reject the liberal support for multiculturalism and openness. Each country in which right-wing populist politicians and movements have attracted support and, in some cases, come to power, has its own history and circumstances shaping its populist phenomenon. In each one, the prospects vary, as do the challenges to the Western idea. For that reason, this analysis looks briefly at the PRR phenomenon in several European countries and then presents a net assessment to conclude the chapter. We start with Western European countries, then move on to those in Eastern and Central Europe. The countries discussed below are included because of the role of PRR politics in them, and the relationship of their circumstances to the broader phenomenon. It is also important to note that PRRs have been generally unsuccessful in some countries. For example, in Romania a combination of PRR clumsiness and centrist expertise has stunted their growth. PRRs are thus not inevitable. The fate of PRRs is the product of conscious decision-making by political leaders, which suggests that they can be defeated through coordinated centrist maneuvering.

France

Summary. France is the most important Western European country that also has an established and relatively popular illiberal party: the National Front (FN – le Front national) led by Marine Le Pen. The FN was formed in 1972 out of a collection of rightist nationalist parties. Its founding head was Jean-Marie Le Pen. His daughter, Marine, took control of the party in 2011. The FN is anti-globalist and anti-immigrant. It wants France to leave both the EU and NATO. It mounted a strong campaign for the presidency in 2017, but lost to Emmanuel Macron, a political novice representing a new party.

Jean-Marie Le Pen established Le Front national in 1972 and his daughter Marine took control of the party 2011. Seeking to "cleanse" the party, she purged many senior FN members and distanced herself from her father, who was expelled from the party in 2015.

This process of cleansing – which she called "de-demonization" – was the first in many steps that Marine Le Pen has taken to reshape and rebrand the FN. The most significant move was to distance the party and her platform from her father's anti-Semitic rhetoric. Anti-Semitism was replaced with radical anti-Islamist, anti-immigration and anti-refugee stances.

After the devastating 2015 Islamist terrorist attack on the offices of the Parisian satirical publication *Charlie Hebdo*, Marine Le Pen offered to help fight the "war that has been declared" on France. But Marine's war on terrorism was only a thinly veiled war on Islam. The uptick in terrorism came alongside Islamophobia, even though two other highly publicized French terrorist attacks were perpetrated by French nationals who justified their violence with right-wing rhetoric. FN nonetheless emphasizes the link between Muslim immigration and political instability: fewer Muslims, fewer terrorists.

In Marine Le Pen's 2017 campaign, she warned of "two totalitarianisms": globalization and Islamism.[7] A short list of her anti-globalist policies is: leave the EU, Eurozone and Schengen Area; restore French "sovereignty"; reduce immigration to 10,000 per year and carry out mass deportations; hire 15,000 new federal police officers; raise taxes on imports; lower domestic taxes; leave NATO's integrated command; limit free education to French citizens only; reassert "French cultural identity." Her campaign slogan was "*On est chez nous*" (This is our country). Le Pen's anti-immigration stances fit perfectly into her populist message, which blames elites and immigrants for longstanding economic problems. Le Pen has masterfully capitalized on economic concerns, promising Trump-esque reindustrialization. Though economic arguments made for a small part of Le Pen's platform, her claim that mainstream parties could not or would not address economic fears brought her overwhelming blue-collar support in the 2017 elections.

Le Pen's le Front national has bragged of a close relationship with Russian president Putin. The FN reportedly received a 9.4 million Euro loan from Russia in November 2014. Le Pen defended the transaction against charges that the loan was a reward for having supported Russia's annexation of Crimea earlier that year. Press sources at the time reported that Le Pen admired Putin as a strong leader.[8] And, in advance of the 2017 presidential voting, Le Pen made an ostentatious visit to Moscow to meet with Putin, receiving support from both Putin and US president Trump.

The way in which the French election played out was highly unusual, as voters chose two "outsiders": Le Pen and Emmanuel Macron, the candidate of the new centrist En Marche! party, to face down in the final round. Though Le Pen lost the election, she garnered 34 percent – over ten million votes. Despite the loss, she has a loyal group of angry followers who view the world through Le Pen's eyes. The French electorate subsequently gave Macron's En Marche! party strong representation in the National Assembly, but Le Pen and the FN will likely remain formidable opponents.

Germany

Summary. The Alternative for Germany (AfD – Alternativ für Deutschland), which came on stage in 2013, is not the first PRR to enter German politics, but it has become the most important one, largely based on the refugee issue. The AfD is the first recognizable party to challenge the liberal and transatlantic order from any part of the German political spectrum. Until the 2017 elections, the AfD seemed to hold only limited political attraction for German voters. The party's surge to prominence was produced almost entirely by lingering public concern about the refugee issue. That issue produced a significant number of votes (12.6 percent) and seats (94) in the Bundestag in the September 2017 national elections.

Why have PRRs generally failed in Germany? Besides the brief-lived Pro-Deutschmark Party, there are three parties that can loosely be grouped under the PRR category. All three have in the past been unsuccessful because the German political elite offered room for nationalists on the center-right while stigmatizing the glorification of the past (i.e. fascism). Thus, no opportunists or moderates had any incentive to join PRRs that glorified the past. The AfD broke through by avoiding the stigma of glorifying the past or, to put it simply, appearing fascist. In contrast to other European countries, German political culture remains allergic to extreme populist appearance.

The AfD's success has been due in part to the fact that its leaders have generally been politically experienced, civicly skilled and seemingly moderate. Thus, they passed the bar for basic acceptance as a player in German politics. Despite its recent success, the AfD is in many ways the least populist of populist radical right parties on the European continent. It also suffers from some serious divisions between moderates and more radical elements. Although the AfD has attempted to avoid the trap of the "single-issue party," if the refugee issue were to become less prominent, the AfD might find itself once again a less significant force in German politics. As in other countries, the success of this PRR has been due to failures of more established parties, and Merkel's success in managing the refugee issue with her new coalition will likely determine the AfD's near-term prospects.

Spain

Summary. As suggested in the German case, Spain's experience with fascism may have played a major role in deterring the growth of modern populist radical right parties. While PRR parties do exist in Spain, they have had very little electoral influence. Since 1980, none of the three leading PRR parties has gained more than 1 percent of a vote. The Democracia Nacional, founded in 1995 by Manuel Canduela Serrano, focuses on a populist nationalism connecting a "Spain First" ideology with common sense voting. España-2000, founded by Rafael Ripoll in 2002, shares many PRR parties' platforms of anti-immigration and tax reform. The more localized Plataforma per Catalunya, founded in 2002 by Josep Anglada, follows a slogan of "Natives first" and is also anti-immigration.

Why have these radical right parties been unsuccessful in capitalizing on anti-immigrant and populist sentiment? The Great Recession hit Spain hard, as unemployment reached a whopping 26 percent in 2013. But, in response, more centrist parties responded in ways that denied grounds on the issue to the radical right. In several localities, Spanish voters saw immigrants as helpful contributors to the economy who were missed when they left Spain in the wake of the recession. Immigrants have not generally been singled out as denying jobs or benefits to Spaniards. Therefore, anti-immigrant sentiment, a cornerstone of PRR rhetoric, has not gained traction. In addition, Spaniards are generally supportive of EU membership and the benefits that that membership entails.

One important influence on the failure of PRRs to gain traction in Spain is likely the bad memory of Spanish fascism. Spanish democracy is only four decades old, and followed four decades of autocratic rule under Francisco Franco. The brutality of the regime left an indelible mark on Spanish politics and society. Few Spanish politicians want to be associated with the regime or its years of political dominance even, or perhaps particularly, at a time when Donald Trump and other radical populists have surged in popularity elsewhere.

The Netherlands

Summary. The banner of the populist radical right has been carried in The Netherlands since 2005 by the Party for Freedom (PVV – Partij Voor de Vrijheid). The party's origins, however, can be traced to television personality and sociology professor Pim Fortuyn, who formed his own party, the Pim Fortuyn List (LPF – Lijst Pim Fortuyn), in 2002.

From its very inception, populist radical rightism in The Netherlands has been based on protecting secular values from a perceived Islamic tide. Fortuyn's entire campaign in the 2002 elections was based on protecting secular Dutch values. Openly gay, Fortuyn embraced liberal democracy and championed freedom of speech and women in need of liberation from Islam. During the election campaign of that year, he was assassinated by an animal rights activist.

Fortuyn's death left a vacuum in Dutch PRR politics. In 2005, Geert Wilders founded the PVV. While a long-term parliamentarian and veteran of Dutch politics, he curated a populist face. To Wilders, Muslim immigrants are seeking to Islamify Europe. The LPF's rhetoric that was the foundation of Fortuyn's brief success left a legacy picked up by the successor PVV. Given that both PRRs achieved their success around the personalities of their founders, it seems that the success of PRR politics in The Netherlands has been at least partly due to cults of personality.

Wilders's ideology is also a bit different from that of other radical right populist leaders. Rather than praise fascists, Wilders describes Islam as comparable to fascism. His arguments seem more focused on protecting so-called Western values, painting himself as a logical successor to the strong men that resisted totalitarianism in Europe's past. Like other PRRs, the PVV bases much of its rhetoric on an anti-elite gospel in addition to its strong anti-Islam philosophy.

In 2017, riding the refugee wave that injected energy into populist parties across the continent, Wilders mounted a strong challenge. But, taking a cue from Angela Merkel, the incumbent prime minister Mark Rutte co-opted far-right rhetoric by arguing that immigrants must respect Dutch values or leave. Rutte's party nonetheless lost seats in the parliament, hanging on as the largest parliamentary party. Wilders's PVV increased its seats in parliament to become the second largest parliamentary party behind Rutte's, setting itself up as a major opposition party, given that no major party was willing to go into coalition with it.

Belgium

Summary. Belgium's Flemish Interest (VB – Vlaams Belang) party (previously called the Vlaams Blok) is quite possibly the most extreme of European PRRs. Until very recently, the party and its base openly espoused anti-Semitic sentiment. The party was even founded by a well-known Holocaust denier. The Vlaams Blok's extremism led to an organized effort by the mainstream parties to shut it down, but this hardline stance increased the view of the VB as a martyr persecuted by the establishment. Non-cooperation nonetheless ensured the VB never entered a coalition government.

Despite its extreme anti-immigrant policies (even for a PRR), the VB was not able to take much advantage of the refugee crisis due to a combination of factional infighting and competition from other PRRs. The Vlaams Blok nonetheless truly terrified the Belgian political establishment.

All mainstream parties signed a *cordon sanitaire* agreement never to cooperate with the VB. While this kept the VB from entering a governing coalition, many believe this non-cooperation policy green-lighted continued VB grassroots growth. In 2004, under a law passed by establishment parties, the high court ruled that the Vlaams Blok was guilty of racist ideology, effectively removing VB access to state funding and shutting down the party. However, the party simply reformed under the new name of Vlaams Belang. At the time of its shut-down, VB had grown to become the most popular political party in Flanders.

Even as the mainstream political parties maneuvered to neutralize the VB, it was experiencing an internal revolution. Filip Dewinter, groomed directly by the VB's founder, began guiding the party in more moderate directions. Rather than championing anti-Semitism, he tried to woo Jewish voters to the VB. The appeal was simple. Instead of scapegoating Jews, Dewinter sought to scapegoat Muslims while appealing to Jews.

Despite moderation of the anti-Semitic message, Dewinter continued the hardline stance of the VB in most other respects. In a seventy-point plan, he argued for denying non-Europeans the right to vote, segregating their children and deporting as many as possible to stem the "Islamic invasion."[9] Nonetheless, the party declined due to factional infighting and the emergence of another PRR, the New Flemish Alliance (N-VA – Nieuw-Vlaamse Alliantie). The N-VA seized 44 percent of the VB's 2010 voters in 2014. Thus, what was once one of the most successful PRRs was largely neutralized at a time when the refugee crisis was providing momentum for most radical right populists.

Austria

Summary. In contrast to Germany and Spain, Austrians are not deeply discomforted with populism or idolization of the past. After World War II, rather than feeling guilty for helping propel Hitler to power, Austrians developed a victim complex that fixates on the "good old days" of the fallen Austro-Hungarian Empire and stresses the country's status as Hitler's "first victim." Many Austrians are relatively comfortable with PRR politics in both mainstream parties and incarnate parties that embody its spirit. As one example, Adolf Schaerf, a socialist candidate for president in 1957, campaigned under the slogan, "Who once voted for Adolf, vote again for Adolf this year." Schaerf won the election. It is evident that PRR politics infected the mainstream even in the immediate aftermath of World War II. This was confirmed in the results of the 2017 parliamentary elections.

Despite this conservative foothold in mainstream Austrian politics, extreme right populists nonetheless still sprouted up. The most notable, the Freedom Party, was founded by former Nazi Anton Reinthaller in 1956. However, the Freedom Party in Austria first reached national prominence in the late 1980s under the leadership of a popular, smiling Jörg Haider. His rhetoric was rife with near-overt and normalized fascist apologism. Among other controversial statements, Haider referred to Hitler's concentration camps as "punishment camps," praised fascist German labor policy and called for reparations for Germans forced out of Czechoslovakia after Hitler's defeat. In the 2000 election some 47 percent of the Austrian working class voted for the Freedom Party.

Haider based his political message on an anti-immigrant (specifically, Balkan) gospel. He embodied the European far right as its most recognizable leader of the era in the way that Marine le Pen does today. Austria's political circumstances – favorable to PRR gaining working-class support – were comparable to the European scene more generally. However, Haider fell out in factional infighting, leaving the party to establish a new and less successful PRR in 2005. He died in an automobile accident in 2008.

The Freedom Party then experienced a brief stagnation until the rise of another designer populist figure, Norbert Hofer. Like Haider, Hofer was a fresh and digital age-savvy face in the sea of establishmentarian Austrian politicians. Under Hofer, Haider's anti-Balkan message became an anti-Islam message. By the first round of the 2016 Austrian presidential election, Hofer had surpassed both mainstream political parties. He was eventually defeated by Alexander van der Bellen, of the Green Party, who was endorsed by both mainstream parties in the third presidential round.

However, the 2017 parliamentary elections demonstrated that failures of the political center combined with mainstream party adoption of PRR-like policies can produce decisive swings toward the populist right. Sebastian Kurz, the young and dynamic leader of the conservative People's Party (ÖVP – Österreichische Volkspartei), a partner in the previous grand coalition government with the Social Democrats (SPÖ – Sozialdemokratische Partei Österreichs), won the opportunity to form the next government with a strongly populist, anti-immigrant platform. At the same time, the Freedom Party came in just behind the Socialists, positioning itself as a coalition partner for Kurz's ÖVP.

Sweden

Summary. The Sweden Democrats (SD – Sverigedemokraterna), founded in 1988, is one of the most prominent populist radical right parties in social democratic bastion Scandinavia. Not surprisingly, SD has recently gained popularity due to its views on immigration policy, specifically in response to the Syrian Civil War and consequent refugee crisis. The rest of its platform sounds identical to other European PRRs: restrict immigration and hold a referendum on EU membership. The SD fosters Eurosceptic sentiments, opposing Turkey joining the EU and blaming EU bureaucrats for "unfair" trade deals. The SD promotes a mercantilist vision of free trade congruent with President Trump's anti-globalization, America First economic platform. As for their anti-immigration platform, the party claims that multiculturalism leads to societal fragmentation and violence – textbook xenophobia.

The party presents itself as a socially conservative, nationalist coalition of anti-immigration and anti-Islamist activists. The SD anti-immigration stance is a populist response to an influx of refugees – the country has granted automatic residence to tens of thousands of Syrian refugees, and in 2014 an estimated 80,000 people applied for asylum.

Though SD claims to be intolerant of racism, its anti-Islamist stance suggests otherwise. Since its founding in 1988, the party has been tarnished by a well-earned racist reputation. Much like France's FN, the SD has been plagued by anti-Semitism. During the 2014 parliamentary election season, one local candidate was photographed wearing a swastika armband. More recently, SD leader and party chairman Jimmie Åkesson called Islam the "Nazism and communism of our time."[10]

The Sweden Democrats in 2017 held 49 of the 349 seats in parliament, having received approximately 13 percent of the vote in the 2014 general elections. All other parties in parliament refused to go into a coalition with SD, due to the party's negative reputation among progressives and moderates alike. The SD has created youth groups to promote its ideology among young voters, building a small but strong bloc of support. SD even has its own news platform – Avipixlat.info – akin to Trump's connections to Breitbart.com. The party holds two seats in the Europe of Freedom and Direct Democracy group, a Eurosceptic group in the European Parliament chaired by the UK's Nigel Farage and comprising members from Italy's Five Star Movement, the British UKIP and the Alternative for Germany.

Switzerland

Summary. Under the leadership of a Trump-like populist billionaire, Christoph Blocher, a center-right agrarian party under the name of the Swiss People's Party (SVP – Schweizerische Volkspartei) was converted into a far-right PRR. Then, by absorbing other fringe parties, the SVP grew to become the largest political party in the country. Under SVP leadership, Switzerland has steered clear from joining the European Union and is on the brink of rupturing the norms of free movement in pursuit of implementing immigration quotas. However, while the SVP is in control of the country, recent referenda illustrate that the direct democratic tradition of Switzerland equips the citizenry to reject SVP policies it does not like without voting the SVP out of office.

The SVP is successful among more disadvantaged classes in Switzerland, largely due to the party's anti-immigrant cultural message rather than economic policy. The SVP achieved its primary policy goal at the time with approval of immigration quotas in a 2014 referendum. This ruptured the EU–Swiss agreement on free movement and the rush of refugees into Europe only further solidified the dominant SVP position. The SVP is nonetheless still negotiating this tense situation and compromising on further legislation to meet EU demands. Despite the SVP's currently dominant position in Swiss politics, its future is not guaranteed. In February 2017, 60.4 percent of Swiss voters voted in a referendum for a path along which third-generation immigrants could reach citizenship. This was against the wishes of the SVP, suggesting that the party could be vulnerable to more open attitudes of the Swiss electorate.

Italy

Summary. The Italian radical right populist movement is primarily represented by the Five Star Movement (M5S – Movimento 5 Stelle) and the Northern League (LN – Lega Nord). Ever since Benito Mussolini's fascist rule (1922–43), the Italian political establishment has failed to answer the most pressing Italian social questions. This has provided the ground for contemporary populist parties. The Five Star Movement boasts the largest political umbrella among European PRRs, attracting leftists as well as rightists. The Northern League is plagued by its history of anti-southern sentiment, which could constrain its future growth.

Both the M5S and LN have deep roots in the long Italian populist tradition. However, while the M5S developed out of the anti-partisan strain of the Italian political impulse, the Lega Nord soared into prominence with its opposition to centralization. Italian fascists (Mussolini) were centralizing, and so a comparison to fascists falls short in describing the LN. The Lega Nord motivated its base by concern that Rome was "stealing" northern money for disproportionate allocation to the south. For this, it blamed the elites in Rome—thus, populism.

Today's Northern League is led by Matteo Salvini, who has kept an orthodox, hard-right policy and criticizes the M5S as "soft" populism. He has begun courting alliances with other PRR leaders around the continent, such as France's Marine le Pen and Geert Wilders in The Netherlands, and has also signed a cooperation deal with Vladimir Putin's party. While other PRRs in Europe take hardline deportation stances against all immigrants, the LN admits that refugees that legally enter should be welcome and provided asylum. But this position is set within a strongly anti-Islam posture. Because Lega Nord developed from an anti-southern and secessionist platform, it will have difficulty ever attracting southern Italian voters, even though they are taking the brunt of the refugee crisis and are thus a logical constituency.

While the Northern League boasts a longer history, the M5S is currently the leading Italian populist party. More than any other PRR, the Five Star Movement capitalized on unrest and dissatisfaction with the Italian establishment and its inability to produce policy that addressed Italian social issues. Started by satirist Beppe Grillo in 2009 from an internet blog, the M5S is one of the largest political parties in Italy. Its origins are uniquely modern, and some would argue that the party cannot be classified as a PRR. In many ways, the M5S takes on a young and left-leaning profile. It proposes sustainable development, improved transportation and environmental regulation. It opposes foreign interventions and proposes an increase in direct democracy and internet freedom. The M5S is distinguished by being more successful than other PRRs in establishing a large populist umbrella inclusive of the left against the establishment. However, its populist character is reflected most clearly in its anti-immigrant stance and disdain for European norms and the EU bureaucracy in Brussels.

In 2013, the M5S was the largest vote-getter in Italy; in 2016, an M5S candidate won the mayoral election in Rome. But while the Five Star Movement is successful, its uniquely large umbrella of all political stripes could be its Achilles heel. The party does not broadcast its anti-immigrant message loudly. The M5S has balked at the prospect of forming a coalition with an establishment party. The Five Star Movement's balancing act toward Russia may prove more difficult as it consents to being courted from the Kremlin despite previous opposition to Putinist corruption. Associating with Putin may be more PRR-like than many of the leftists under the M5S's umbrella would like.

Greece

Summary. Radical right-wing populism has taken a particularly violent and emboldened form in Greece. Golden Dawn (Chryssa Avgi) was founded in 1980, led by Nikolaos Michaloliakos. This party, long considered neo-Nazi, features a two-pronged platform based on anti-immigration and anti-austerity measures, and has been associated with the commission of many hate crimes.

In response to the Greek economic crisis in 2012, Golden Dawn opposed involvement in multilateral institutions such as the International Monetary Fund, European Union and European Central Bank. It emphasized anti-immigration stances to distinguish itself from other, more radical Greek parties like the leftist Syriza. Golden Dawn is also unique among PRR parties because its economic policies are geared toward stronger government involvement, so long as bailouts are limited. Given this overlap with the more mainstream parties, its stances have gained some public acceptance and it has been able to use a mainstream agenda to its advantage. While its platform is not particularly religiously grounded, Golden Dawn has pursued relationships with the Greek Orthodox Church to expand its voter base. But it differs from the church on ties to the military and police force influenced by the party's admiration for Ioannis Metaxas, Greek prime minister, general and dictator from 1936 to 1941.

Golden Dawn not only tolerates violence, but also openly encourages it as a means of solidifying political power. In 2012, a majority of the 154 recorded hate crime attacks in Greece were attributed to the organization. The highly publicized killing of left-wing hip-hop artist Pavlos Fyssas by a self-identified Golden Dawn member inspired by the party's message led to mass anti-fascism protests, and the realization that Golden Dawn's influence extended beyond that of a mere political coalition.

Golden Dawn gained influence leading up to the 2010 Athens local elections. Feeling disenfranchised and resentful of immigrants who were seen as contributing to cramped, poor living conditions in the city's interior, Athenian citizens turned toward new options. Golden Dawn's influence faded somewhat after the murder of Fyssas, but in the 2015 elections, after another bailout, support rose again.

More recently, the Brexit referendum and Donald Trump's election seemed to have emboldened Golden Dawn. In 2016 and early 2017 the party remained the third largest in the country, with 10 percent of the popular vote, continuing to emphasize its anti-immigrant nationalist approach. In January 2017, Golden Dawn members took to the streets of Athens to protest the Greek government's lack of a Trump-style immigration ban. Greece has been struck particularly hard by the global refugee crisis given its economic hardships and geographic proximity to refugee flows, and Golden Dawn has taken advantage of the atmosphere of uncertainty and fear to advance its platform. Economic prospects for the average Greek remain dismal and, as refugees continue to tax Greece's economy, this unpredictable and resilient party could rise even higher.

Hungary

Summary. While it began as a college dorm-based party championing minority rights and secularism, Hungarian Civic Alliance

(Fidesz – Magyar Polgári Szövetség), Hungary's ruling party led by Prime Minister Viktor Orban, has most of the traits of a populist radical right party. Fidesz is radically nationalistic, anti-immigrant and anti-elite.

Fidesz's turn to the right can best be explained by the natural democratic tendency to trend toward a two-party system combined with the opportunism of its most prominent founder. Viktor Orban, previously known as a firebrand against communism, convinced the youthful party to abandon its consensus-based model to adopt an executive structure with Orban on top. Orban then positioned Fidesz to take up the mantle as the dominant right-leaning opposition. The party began to emphasize God and country while decrying elites. The party became the "most centralized, most homogeneous, and most disciplined party in the country."[11] Under Orban, constitutionalism is not only threatened but refugees have also suffered some of the worst persecution in Europe. This violence has been government-sanctioned and deliberate to support Fidesz power, and even more extreme groups are enabled by Orban's PRR politics.

While Fidesz has become for all intents and purposes a PRR, it is traditionally classified simply as "conservative." Its extremist policies – which are more radical than certain other "real" PRRs, like the Swiss People's Party – and its strategy align with PRR politics. However, Orban has recently faced opposition not from the opposition socialists but from the far right. The Movement for a Better Hungary (Jobbik) is a hardline PRR that more closely matches the academic definition of the term. If in power, it would be less adept at implementing its radical policies than the ruling Fidesz due to inexperience, despite having more extreme policies on Jews and Roma in addition to immigrants in general.

Czech Republic

Summary. The Czech Republic's political relationship with the populist threat is not adequately captured by the PRR framework. While PRRs exist, none of the leading parties is purely PRR. But the Czech political "mainstream" embodies many of the characteristics of the populist radical right. While most Western European mainstream parties date back decades or even centuries, Eastern European mainstream parties are as young as Western European PRRs (some, even younger). The Czech Republic's current president, Milos Zeman, emerged in this setting and his Social Democratic Party has adopted PRR-friendly policies.

In 1989, Vaclav Havel led Czechoslovakia out of communism. After Czechoslovakia split into the Czech Republic and Slovakia in 1993, Milos Zeman guided the Social Democratic Party to the position, at the time, as the leading political party of the Czech Republic. The party champions the welfare state, progressive taxation and equitability. However, Zeman's own personality has had a great influence over the party. In 2013, he became the first directly elected president of the Czech Republic, and began adopting some of the most extreme PRR rhetoric. In an interview, Zeman argued that the Czech Republic could be the victim of a jihad or "super-Holocaust." He argued that ordinary, non-practicing Muslims could become radicalized, "fanatic Nazis," just as ordinary Germans in the lead-up to the rise of Nazism. Zeman even described Islam itself as an "inferior part of mankind" and a "religion of death."[12] He stole PRR rhetoric and installed it in the leftist party of the Czech Republic.

The 2017 parliamentary elections were won by the center-right populist party ANO 2011, led by anti-establishment billion-aire Andrej Babiš, with Zeman's Social Democrats falling to sixth place. The ANO 2011 came to prominence largely based on its pledge to fight government corruption. While it too has co-opted some populist policies, it is by no means a PRR.

Co-optation, combined with high court rulings that ban traditional PRRs, has effectively hindered their development. Nonetheless, co-optation has led the Czech mainstream, for all intents and purposes, to reflect influences from the populist radical right.

Poland

Summary. In many respects, contemporary Polish politics revolve around the same nationalist axis as they have for centuries. Poland's Law and Justice (PiS – Prawo i Sprawiedliwość) party is a populist radical right party with traditional Polish characteristics and a strong cult of personality. Unlike other PRRs, Law and Justice remains anti-Russian and not enamored with Putinism. However, the PiS has increasingly adopted policy approaches of other European PRR parties, supplementing anti-elitism with a recognizable anti-refugee message. Most importantly, the PiS currently is Poland's governing party and has been progressively moving away from Western democratic practices.

In Poland, politics is a battle over the very meaning of the nation. Polish nationalism is distinct and more potent than that of most other countries. Polish identity became permanently revolutionary in response to the division of Poland by three countries during the eighteenth century. Since then, the Polish people have been motivated and politicized by various understandings of the nation. However, the umbrella of nationalism always held two bitterly divided constituencies. To some, Poland has meant republican and European since before even the fall of the country in the eighteenth century; to others, Poland meant the glorification of "indigenous" and "native" things. This same division manifested when the umbrella of Polish nationalism was torn in two following the 1989 victory of the Solidarity movement over the communist regime. The two political parties that emerged – Law and Justice and the more centrist Civic Platform (PO – Platforma Obywatelska) – both draw on the centuries-old national constituencies. Thus, it is no surprise that Law and Justice employs its version of Poland as its primary political instrument against the opposition. In May 2016, the PiS government convened an "audit" that amounted to an indictment of the PO for betraying the nation.

The bitter partisan attack on the PO was not surprising. Shortly after Lech Kaczynski's death along with many other senior Polish officials in a plane crash in Russia, his brother (and party boss) organized a campaign to suggest that the PO, in power at the time, was responsible for his death. The PO and PiS do not have dramatically different economic or social policies. But they have very different perspectives on the meaning of Polish nationhood and the best governing approach for Poland's future. PiS ideology rejects what it sees as nihilistic liberal Western values, favored by PO, that PiS believes reflect a secular influence and a rejection of religious and moral principles that define Polishness. Very few PRR ideologies are quite as anti-Western, in that respect, as the Polish variety.

To understand the Law and Justice party, one must understand Jaroslaw Kaczynski. Kaczynski has acted as undisputed boss of the party in its turn toward illiberalism. Yet, paradoxically, he was at the forefront in the movement for democracy. Kaczynski served as secretary for Solidarity leader Lech Walesa himself, and stuck with him longer than most former Solidarity leaders. However, he was never fully accepted by Solidarity. Kaczynski's departure may have been a result of feeling betrayed by Walesa and Solidarity. Not only did they reduce his role, but they forgave former communists and permitted their entrance to the government instead of taking a hardline anti-communist exclusion policy. Kaczynski was furious. His move to PRR politics was built on the foundation of virulent anti-communism.

Through its anti-elite populism combined with potent nationalism, the Law and Justice party soared to success. In 2005, Jaroslaw's brother won the presidency. Jaroslaw himself became prime minister the next year. Civic Platform returned to power in 2007 and rode a period of economic success until Law and Justice ousted it in elections in 2015. Since that time, Law and Justice has been solidifying its control and, according to many observers, replacing Western values and institutions with illiberal approaches to government, education and science, based on the party's PRR policies and substantial support in the electorate.

Law and Justice found new strength from the same source

as other PRR parties, employing explicitly anti-refugee rhetoric as the refugee crisis deepened. The anti-refugee policy is layered on top of a strong appeal to traditional Polish nationalism and conservative religious and social values. The strongest "Western" plank in the party's program – and one that distinguishes Polish radical right populism from most other such parties – is strong skepticism regarding Russia and Putin and support for Poland's NATO membership.

Immigration issues as key stimuli for the populist rise

The most prominent recent source and stimulus for PRR support indeed seems to be immigration and issues related to it. The recent surge of refugees from the war-torn Middle East has put dramatic new focus on the existing concerns related to visa-free movement of people inside the EU's Schengen zone. This is evident not only in Western Europe, but also increasingly in Eastern Europe as the refugee crisis has been utilized by traditionally anti-minority PRRs to boost support. Many Eastern Europeans are dissatisfied not only with the post-communist transformation, but also with immigrants.

In a way, the refugee crisis has homogenized the radical right in Europe. This is potentially dangerous for more liberal and centrist parties, given the widespread push among PRRs to form a cohesive alliance, whose emergence has been encouraged by Russian president Putin's interventions. The concerns over immigrants are, for all intents and purposes, universal. The exceptions where the PRR's main source of appeal examined here seems until recently to have failed are: Germany (with the current strengthening of the PRR Alternative for Germany catalyzed by the large number of refugees welcomed by the German government); Spain, where Franco's legacy has left a strong anti-fascist political culture; and Romania, where the fact that the country has been more a source than recipient of irregular migration has reduced the prominence of the issue.

The widespread public opposition toward taking in refugees, whether due to economic or social concerns, has translated into limited political will throughout the EU to cooperate in dealing with the refugee crisis. This resistance to accepting refugees has led to overcrowding in border states, including Italy and Greece, neither of which are financially able to support refugee resettlement in their country.

Right-wing, fear-mongering populism, seen in so many of the countries surveyed here, prevents a unified and potentially more effective EU-wide or transatlantic approach from coming together. The EU members promised in 2015 to resettle 160,000 refugees from Italy and Greece, but as of March 2017, only about 10 percent of that number had been resettled. Not only does this ambivalence, and sometimes even animosity, toward easing the crisis severely weaken the economies of countries forced to host refugees waiting for resettlement elsewhere throughout the EU, but it also undermines the values that the West holds most dear. Syrian refugees, for example, are fleeing every day from horrific human rights abuses such as airstrikes or chemical weapons and undergoing extremely dangerous and expensive crossings as they are smuggled across the Mediterranean, only to be turned away or held indefinitely at the external borders of the European Union.

Until now, centrist responses to the populist radical right challenge have fallen into two categories: co-optation and non-cooperation. The most common response of mainstream parties to advances of the populist radical right has been the former – adopting rightist rhetoric to hijack support from PRRs. The best example of successful co-optation is found in The Netherlands, where incumbent prime minister Mark Rutte tried to limit the advance of Geert Wilders by adopting his own populist rhetoric. Co-optation possesses significant risk, however. There are more examples of countries where the mainstream willingly adopted far-right politics– Hungary, Poland, Czech Republic, Switzerland – than there are start-up success stories.

The United States can also be understood as a failed

co-optation attempt. The Republican Party granted a platform to the Tea Party, and by doing so the moderates lost control of the party apparatus. Since, the party has floundered and fallen to figures like Donald Trump. This has become even worse, as Donald Trump has implicitly greenlighted (in the same way that Poland's Kaczynski and Hungary's Orban have) the most extreme right in the streets – the alt-right. Co-optation also grants PRRs some power in the indirect sense of influence. By co-opting, moderates put radical ideas into the credible mainstream.

A rare, but more successful, strategy to deal with PRRs has been non-cooperation. In Belgium, PRR parties have remained out of power due to the signing of the *cordon sanitaire* by the mainstream – a commitment never to cooperate with the radical right. This does lead to martyrdom of the radicals, but it has also kept them and their policies from controlling or influencing policy, norms or systems. Whether this strategy will work only under specific circumstances remains to be seen. Perhaps combined with a strong revitalization of the political center, through new policies and new ideas, non-cooperation is the most effective strategy to combat the radical right.

The reality is that, at this point, centrist political forces have not yet found the silver bullet to deal with the surge in populist radical right movements. Their strength has grown based on the refugee crisis on top of a general malaise created by social, economic and governance issues.

In Chapter 7 we consider the challenge for the political center to respond effectively to the conditions that have given rise to the populist radical right. But for now, we turn to Turkey's journey away from its Western moorings.

Notes

1 Jan-Werner Müller, *What is Populism?* (Philadelphia, PA: University of Pennsylvania Press, 2016).

2 Roger Cohen, "The Trump possibility," www.nytimes.com/2016/10/04/opinion/the-trump-possibility.html?_r=0 [accessed 29 April 2017].

3 Richard Rorty, *Achieving Our Country: Leftist Thought in Twentieth-Century America* (Cambridge, MA: Harvard University Press, 1998).

4 Amy B. Wang, "One group loved Trump's remarks about Charlottesville: white supremacists," www.washingtonpost.com/news/post-nation/wp/2017/08/13/one-group-loved-trumps-remarks-about-charlottesville-white-supremacists/?utm_term=.1cce18d81562, [accessed 6 October 2017].

5 K. A. Hawkins, *Venezuela's Chavismo and Populism in Comparative Perspective* (Cambridge: Cambridge University Press, 2010).

6 Cas Mudde, *Populist Radical Right Parties in Europe* (Cambridge: Cambridge University Press, 2007).

7 Adam Nossiter, "Marine Le Pen echoes Trump's bleak populism in French campaign kickoff," *New York Times*, 5 February 2017, www.nytimes.com/2017/02/05/world/europe/marine-le-pen-trump-populism-france-election.html [accessed 4 November 2017].

8 Michelle Martin, "France's Le Pen says she admires Putin as much as Merkel," *Reuters*, 1 June 2014, www.reuters.com/article/us-france-lepen/frances-le-pen-says-she-admires-putin-as-much-as-merkel-magazine-idUSKBN0EC1ES20140601 [accessed 4 November 2017].

9 Gregory Crouch, "Three to watch: populists of the hard right," *New York Times*, 21 April 1996, sec. Magazine, www.nytimes.com/1996/04/21/magazine/three-to-watch-populists-of-the-hard-right.html [accessed 4 November 2017].

10 Fatma Naib, "Sweden immigrants dismayed by far-right gain," 2017, www.aljazeera.com/indepth/features/2014/09/sweden-immigrants-dismayed-far-right-gain-201492172148992275.html [accessed 6 October 2017].

11 Takis S. Pappas, "Populist democracies: post-authoritarian Greece and post-communist Hungary," *Government and Opposition* 49, no. 1 (January 2014), 11.

12 Robert Tait, "Miloš Zeman: the hardline Czech leader fanning hostility to refugees," *The Guardian*, 14 September 2016, sec. World news, www.theguardian.com/world/2016/sep/14/milos-zeman-czech-leader-refugees [accessed 4 November 2017].

4

Turkey's drift away from its Western moorings

Talking Turkey

Since NATO's inception, there has been a tension in the alliance as to what is necessary to provide for the common defense and what is required to translate the implicitly shared values of democracy, individual liberty and the rule of law into national policies. This tension was illustrated early on when, due to the strategic importance of the Azores for US military access to Europe, Portugal was admitted to the alliance despite its autocratic dictatorship, later overturned by the massive Carnation Revolution. At various times since 1949, alliance members Turkey and Greece have gone off the democratic track, with military regimes replacing elected governments. Turkey entered modern history in 1922 via a military coup led by Mustafa Kemal Atatürk and his fellow army officers who pushed the Ottoman Empire and its sultan-caliph into oblivion. Its 1924 Constitution declared the Republic of Turkey to be democratic and secular. Atatürk became its first president and ensured its inclination was to the West. The Turkish military came to perceive itself as successor to Atatürk's "Young Turks" and Guardian of its Democracy. The army has intervened and taken control of the government four times since Turkey joined NATO in 1952: in 1960, 1971, 1980 and 1997.

As one of the countries that has struggled with NATO's value-driven norms, Turkey today is most in danger of violating them. This development is particularly threatening because

Turkey has become a pivotal player on NATO's southeastern flank and the bridge between Europe, the Middle East and Islam. Ankara is also an important participant in the fight against international terrorism and has accepted the largest number of refugees from Syria, Iraq, Afghanistan and Africa (3.4 million as of October 2017).

The secular, pro-Western state that dates to Atatürk's reforms starting with the Constitution of 1924, was substantially modified by an April 2017 national referendum called by President Recep Tayyip Erdoğan. Its popular approval, by a small margin, gives considerably more power to the presidency at the expense of the parliament and judiciary, and this referendum is seen by many as the first step toward the creation of a Putin-style regime under Erdoğan's control. The question is whether and how the West can encourage Turkey to hold to Western values while continuing to serve significant alliance interests in the region.

The abortive relationship between Turkey and the EU may have been a causal factor in Turkey's recent move away from democracy, but European NATO members and the United States will be challenged to try to coax Turkey back into a more democratic and secular path and away from closer relationships with Moscow and Middle Eastern authoritarian regimes. That being said, President Erdoğan's deep commitment to his Sunni beliefs, to reducing the influence of the Kurdish minority both domestically and abroad, and to restoring lost imperial influence must also be taken into account. As conservative Islamists increase their power, Erdoğan has embraced a new domestic religiosity, for example by allowing women in the armed forces to wear hijab and catering to other moderate Islamic nations. He has also expressed a desire for Muslim nations to band together to fight terrorism and increase cohesion within the Islamic world. While this message itself is not necessarily troubling, some in the West suspect the Turkish position has more to do with its struggle against Kurdish separatists and regime opponents than gaining support for Western counterterrorist policies.

Turkey's shifting external alignments

As a member of NATO since 1952, Turkey should value Western ideals and, indeed, millions of its citizens do. However, President Erdoğan is pursuing a different agenda that calls into question its commitment to the West and suggests that Turkey may be moving toward new positions both domestically and internationally that could estrange it from the transatlantic community.

NATO has relied on Turkey as an outpost for Western principles in an area surrounded by contending beliefs and undemocratic governments. With a military ranking second only to the United States in numbers of military personnel, Turkey historically has been an important NATO contributor. But Turkey's interest in participating in NATO has waned in the last two years as little progress has been registered in its twelve-year EU-entry negotiations. In 2016, it participated in just four of NATO's eighteen multinational joint exercises. Moreover, its post-2016 coup purges have seriously damaged its position in the alliance and in the broader Euro-American collaboration.

Since the EU accession talks began, there have been those in the EU that believed Turkey could never qualify for membership. Most recently, the Turkey–EU relationship has been driven largely by the refugee crisis. A 2016 deal between the European Commission and Turkey established a one-for-one refugee resettlement agreement – for every refugee resettled within Europe, one must be resettled in Turkey up to a cap of 72,000 – in exchange for some $6-plus billion over 2016, 2017 and 2018, to care for them, along with promises of progress on EU accession talks and visa-free travel for Turkish citizens in the EU. Today, Turkey hosts 3.4 million refugees, prompting its nickname of "Europe's warehouse for migrants." While the stream into Europe has subsequently slowed, Turkey's demands for visa-free travel never led to EU policy changes. Having seen very limited returns from the deal, President Erdoğan threatened to withdraw Turkey's EU accession bid. Regardless, his departure from democratic norms and military operations in Syria against Syrian Kurds, US allies against ISIL, have likely already frozen prospects for further progress toward EU membership.

Meanwhile, Ankara has actively pursued closer working relationships with Russia and Islamic nations, including Iran. Frustrations with the stalled EU negotiations have served as one of the motivations – or excuses – for Erdoğan to pursue closer ties with Russia, despite recent serious tensions with Moscow. Visits to Ankara by the chiefs of the Iranian and Russian general staffs indicate that they have overcome tensions caused by Turkey's 2015 downing of a Russian fighter that allegedly violated Turkey's airspace and the 2016 assassination of Russia's ambassador to Turkey. President Putin recognizes that Turkey's current path creates openings for improved relations between the two countries and weakening ties to NATO and Europe. Erdoğan appreciates the leverage and support he thus gains against his Western critics. At the 2017 World Economic Forum in Davos, Switzerland, Turkish deputy prime minister Mehmet Simsek suggested Turkey would be interested in participating in diplomatic meetings with Russia and Iran regarding a ceasefire in Syria. Then, poking a thumb in NATO's eye, Turkey in July 2017 reportedly reached an agreement with Moscow to purchase as well as co-produce a major Russian anti-aircraft defense missile system.

Ankara has also expressed a willingness to work with moderate Islamic regimes, including Tehran. President Erdoğan seems to be transitioning from Atatürk's 1924 secularism toward a kind of Sunni-Islam-fueled nationalism, seeking to retrieve some of the Ottoman Empire's former stature in the Islamic world.

This perceived drift away from the West is deeply rooted in domestic Turkish politics. Ethnic (Turkmen vs. Kurdish) and party tensions have been rising for several years, leading to a failed *coup d'état* against the Erdoğan government, subsequent purges, and a constitutional referendum designed to deepen his and his party's control of the nation as well as its Islamization.

Domestic tensions

While Turkey claims to be a multi-partisan democracy, Erdoğan's Justice and Development Party (AKP – Adalet ve Kalkınma Partisi) has in sixteen years gone from holding a handful of parliamentary seats to its current position as the overwhelmingly predominant force in national politics. It has won twelve consecutive elections and been in power for fifteen of its sixteen years of existence. It lost its majority in the June 2015 elections but won it back in a snap election later that year. Erdoğan served as prime minister for several years before being elected president in 2014. His and his party's rise to virtual national control was initially accepted because of the country's economic success between 2002 and 2016 (2008 recession excepted). Turkey's GDP and standard of living increased significantly while its European neighbors struggled.

The AKP's success did not mean that it was entirely unopposed. Both the Republican People's Party (CHP – Cumhuriyet Halk Partisi) and the People's Democratic Party (HDP – Halkların Democratik Partisi) were vocal opponents of many AKP policies. They remained represented in parliament as well, with a notable 2015 HDP surge.

However, given the much-enlarged presidential powers following the 2017 referendum, the post-coup state of emergency which conferred extrajudicial arrest and detention authority on the executive, and the jailing of HDP deputies, active parliamentary opposition was reduced dramatically.

Clashes between the AKP and HDP go beyond mere ideological differences. The HDP has long been sympathetic to the Kurdistan Workers' Party (PKK – Partiya Karkerên Kurdistanê). Starting in the 1980s, the PKK has fought a bloody insurrection against Ankara (40,000 Kurdish civilians killed), demanding independence or autonomy. The Turkish government long ago branded the PKK, and Kurds in general, terrorists and enemies of the state.

The US government, the European Union and NATO initially (1990s) accepted that "terrorist" caption. However, following renewed Turkish assaults on domestic Kurds in 2015, later expanded to include Syrian and Iraqi Kurdish allies of the US-led anti-ISIL coalition, that label is being questioned.

The tipping point

In 2004 Prime Minister Erdoğan enjoyed great popularity, providing strong leadership while helping revive the Turkish economy. The AKP was gaining strength and Erdoğan was talking and acting like a Western-leaning Atatürkian secularist. Then-US ambassador to Turkey, Eric Edelman, wrote a cable describing "Erdoğan's 'overbearing pride,' 'unbridled ambition,' 'authoritarian loner streak,' and 'overweening desire to stay in power.'" Still, the cable went on to conclude that despite these manifest faults, Erdoğan was, at the time, "the only partner capable of advancing toward the U.S. vision of a successful, democratic Turkey integrated into Europe."[1] Edelman, despite ultimately being too optimistic, may have put his finger on the future when he described Erdoğan's pride, ambition and authoritarian tendencies.

Starting in 2012–13, Erdoğan and the AKP felt strong enough to challenge the military and the opposition parties directly. Much like Trump and many PRR leaders, Erdoğan appealed over their heads to the people, claiming he and the AKP were victims of the entrenched elite. It worked. His popular support rose sharply and enabled more power to be quietly moved to the executive. However, not all Turks accepted Erdoğan's growing authoritarianism. In 2013, a large anti-government protest took place in Istanbul's Gezi Park, sparking a very violent response and producing international outrage. Then, in 2015, Erdoğan ignored his 2013 peace deal with Kurdish leader Ocalan (in prison) and the Kurds, and ordered the military to resume their operations against them.

Three years later, in the summer of 2016, a group of Turkish military officers, with some backing from the national army, attempted a *coup d'état* against Erdoğan's government. The coup leaders claimed to be acting like the Turkish military had in the past, intervening to save secular democracy. The trigger may possibly have been Erdoğan's rumored plan to remove many senior officials, allegedly for ties to his former partner and now arch-critic, Fetullah Gülen, a very well-known cleric exiled to the United States, where he is a permanent resident alien living in Pennsylvania. Ultimately, the coup failed because senior officials condemned the plotters and Erdoğan used social media to call on the public to protest in the streets.

The Turkish government immediately claimed the coup attempt had been orchestrated by Gülen and his supporters, demanding that the United States extradite Gülen to Turkey. To date, Washington has refused, stating Ankara had provided no direct evidence of his involvement. Moreover, blaming Gülen for the attempted overthrow was not accepted by most objective observers because several senior participants in the coup attempt had condemned Gulen's movement, and perceived themselves as protectors of the Turkish Republic. Others have suggested that Erdoğan himself had contrived the coup with hopes of emerging victorious as a strong and devoted leader, but there is little evidence to support this theory.[2]

Whatever the truth, Erdoğan wasted no time in applying an iron fist, jailing tens of thousands of civil servants, military officers, academics and journalists, and shuttering dozens of media outlets. Within weeks he confiscated corporations, arrested mayors and ordered hundreds of officials stationed overseas to return to Turkey. Many sought asylum in the host countries.

His actions alarmed the Obama administration and many European and other democratic governments and publics. While Erdoğan claimed that the state of emergency he imposed was "not against democracy, the rule of law and freedom," his actions suggested the opposite.[3] Internationally, many countries and the United Nations condemned his "purge" as gross violations of human rights. Four-plus months after the purges began, the EU parliament formally adjourned its membership discussions with Turkey.

Constitutional referendum

In 2016, President Erdoğan proposed a constitutional referendum, allegedly to address concerns about terrorism (there were more than ten major explosions in large Turkish cities in 2016), the economy and supposed government weakness, but clearly designed to enhance his control of national decision-making. The proposed constitutional reforms had already failed in the parliament, so Erdoğan sought to give the changes democratic legitimacy through the referendum. The constitutional changes would give Erdoğan and the AKP an even more dominant place in Turkish governance. The proposed changes would draw power away from the parliament and allow closer relationships between the office of the president and the majority party. It would severely limit the office of prime minister, making the president the sole spokesperson for the national government. It would permit extension of the state of emergency declared after the coup attempt, allowing additional control of the media and individual surveillance. It also could allow Erdoğan to remain in power until 2029 – a disturbing prospect considering his ever-increasing tendency toward authoritarian rule. The referendum won a narrow 51.4 percent to 48.6 percent victory. That slim win, combined with allegations of election fraud and disproportionate media coverage of the "Yes" camp, suggested that Erdoğan was less than beloved by his people and was trying to use the referendum – a supposed instrument of democracy – to strengthen his grip on power. His tactic of maintaining a veneer of representative government may suggest awareness of Western concerns about his undemocratic moves. Erdoğan denies an attempt to become leader for life, but the new powers granted by the referendum have provided good cause to fear that he could well be putting Turkish democracy on a slippery slope.

What now?

Domestically, the response to Erdoğan's strategy has reflected the national divisions suggested by the referendum outcome. In the summer of 2017, thousands of protesters participated in a three-week "March for Justice" from Ankara to Istanbul. Headed by Kemal Kiliçdaroğlu of the opposing CHP, the march demanded transparency and adherence to fair, democratic processes in the wake of the post-coup purge and referendum. The march culminated in a one million-strong rally in Istanbul that emphasized the need for real justice and challenged Erdoğan to be more transparent.

Given the violent response to protesters in Gezi Park in 2013 and lack of any significant negative political consequences for Erdoğan as a result, many watched the march unfold with bated breath, wondering when the national police would be called to violently disperse the crowd. However, the march and rally concluded peacefully. Erdoğan was careful not to make Kiliçdaroğlu into a hero and, by allowing the march to conclude, he displayed a veneer of democratic behavior. In addition to giving popular voice in response to a potentially fraudulent vote, the march and rally showed how much the situation in Turkey had deteriorated since the coup attempt. Almost a year earlier, Erdoğan had conducted a rally of approximately one million people to celebrate the national unity and democracy that had ended the coup. Ironically, the 2017 rally emphasized Erdoğan's failings in those very areas. The people had lost trust in his government's leadership and were concerned that the Justice and Development Party was not living up to its name.

The longer-term international consequences of the referendum's result will depend to some extent on how Erdoğan uses his new presidential powers. But the most likely outcome will be to increase tensions between Turkey and its Western allies as well as domestic tensions. The apparent move toward a more authoritarian, illiberal government structure with power transferred to the executive is incompatible with Western ideals of democracy and the rule of law. Erdoğan's post-coup purges also threaten to weaken Turkey's military and thus the security of NATO. Many officers assigned to NATO were recalled and presumably many who returned to Turkey have ended up in jail, including as much as a third of Turkey's officer corps. Some officers on NATO duty sought asylum in NATO countries to escape that fate.

In the foreseeable future, it would be nearly impossible to resume EU accession negotiations unless Erdoğan shifts dramatically back toward open democracy, and there is no sign he is so disposed. However, so long as the EU is willing to pursue a strong economic partnership with Turkey, that may be enough from Erdoğan's perspective. The chances that Turkey would finally win EU membership were already in the slim-to-none category. Turkey nonetheless has an interest in keeping trade and economic doors open to Europe, and will undoubtedly use whatever leverage it can muster to protect its economic interests. Erdoğan, in the meantime, can use the refugee relationship with Europe and his flirtation with Putin and Islamic regimes to maintain leverage. One scholar has suggested that Ankara is now interested in economic partnerships with Western countries and organizations, but no longer wants to adhere to its political norms.[4] If so, is this compatible with Turkey's membership in NATO? How will the West reconcile its basic values with the political necessity of sustaining at a minimum, partnership with Erdoğan's regime?

The coup and referendum have also shown Turkey's desire to re-orient its international relations by moving away from multilateralism and toward bilateral partnerships with major powers such as the United States, China or Russia. No longer seriously seeking EU membership, Turkey is instead testing the limits of its allies, neighbors and other powers. Ankara is aware of its bargaining power on the transatlantic stage as a member with great geostrategic relevance, and is taking advantage of the opportunity to advance its agenda, even if to the frustration of its NATO allies.

As Turkey hovers on the geographical and ideological edge of the West, its Kurdish tensions are also influencing NATO relationships. The terrorist classification for the PKK has caused frictions throughout the Middle East, as PKK affiliates have been instrumental in helping the United States and its NATO allies deal with security challenges in the region. In Syria, the United States has been arming the People's Protection Units (YPG – Yekîneyên Parastina Gel) to aid in the fight against Russia-backed Syrian president and dictator Bashar al-Assad. Turkey has strongly condemned the US partnership with the YPG, even though the alternative could be a victory for Assad and, by extension, Russia. Ankara's opposition to accepting the YPG as an ally in the Syria conflict produced a huge rift between Turkey and the United States. President Trump's determination to continue arming the YPG led Erdoğan to look toward other nations – Russia in particular – for support. The continued warming of Erdoğan's relationship with Russian president Putin has raised even more questions about Turkey's future commitment to NATO.

Turkey's spat with Germany also had both practical and symbolic implications. Turkey's Incirlik Air Base provides critical access for the militaries of NATO countries to crisis zones in Syria, northern Africa and the Arabian Peninsula, and is a major base of operations for the US-led coalition against ISIL. As of July 2017, Germany was determined to remove its forces from the base, relocating them to Jordan in response to Turkish refusal to allow German politicians, some of whom were pro-PKK, to visit Incirlik.[5] Ankara and Berlin had previously exchanged harsh criticisms, and Berlin took this event as the last straw. The German decision to move forces from a fellow NATO member state to a non-member chilled relations with Turkey to the bone. This disagreement will force Ankara to make some difficult choices. Germany is Turkey's largest trading partner, is home for nearly three million Turks and leads most EU negotiations with Turkey. Turkey likely cannot afford to lose Germany. Moreover, troubled ties with the United States, including US failure to deport Fetullah Gülen as demanded by Erdoğan, could help Erdoğan's domestic opposition make the case that his government is putting Turkey's national security at risk.

Turkey's pursuit of a unilateral international strategy and authoritarian domestic approach to governance continue to encourage its drift away from the West. Erdoğan seems no longer invested in EU membership or even cooperation without major reciprocal benefits. Turkish officials are quick to call out NATO hypocrisy and point out NATO members' internal struggles when allies discuss Erdoğan's authoritarian streak. On the other side, NATO and the EU want to avoid the impression that they condone Erdoğan's domestic policy, and so they have kept up criticism but avoided a complete rupture of relations.

The bottom line

At a time when the West is facing both external threats and internal challenges, Turkey is moving progressively from being a vitally important geostrategic partner nation to a liability and potentially a threat itself. The Turkish case is different from all other cases of illiberal advances among Western democracies. Turkey has passed through undemocratic periods before and come out with restoration of Western-style democracy. Perhaps that will happen again. However, Turkey's turn toward a more authoritarian style of governance comes at a time when many EU and NATO members, including the United States, hoped that a secular Turkey would prove that a majority Muslim state could still be a strong example on which other Islamic state governments might be modeled.

From a strategic perspective, Turkey has been the tip of the West's spear in the Middle East. But the drift that President Erdoğan is piloting away from Western democratic norms is not only creating divisions among NATO allies but also suggests that Turkey could be the first NATO ally to leave the alliance, perhaps even allying with Russia. This would be a huge loss to NATO's strategic position in the region as well as to the West's demonstration of the validity of its political model.

Turkey, therefore, has become an important part of the problem of illiberalism as a threat to the principles and practice of Western liberal democracy. President Erdoğan shows all the traits of an emerging authoritarian leader, and he has used populist political appeals to keep much of the population pacified. The fact that there still is political opposition to his regime suggests that Turkey is not yet a lost cause. But it certainly is part of the challenge for those who hope to save the West, its institutions and its interests from illiberal threats.

With the Turkish trauma looming on Europe's southeastern flank, we now turn to another country that is on the verge of leaving one of the West's core institutions. We are talking, of course, about Brexit, the British departure from the European Union that was narrowly mandated by a 2016 popular referendum.

Notes

1   Quoted in Nick Danforth, "Tutored by the tragedy of Turkish democracy," Warontherocks.com, 7 March 2017, https://warontherocks.com/2017/03/tutored-by-the-tragedy-of-turkish-democracy/ [accessed 24 August 2017].

2   Aaron Stein, "'Take to the streets': Turkey's failed coup one year later," *Warontherocks.com*, 14 July 2017, https://warontherocks.com/2017/07/take-to-the-streets-turkeys-failed-coup-one-year-later/ [accessed 26 July 2017].

3   Kareem Shaheen, "Turkey coup attempt: Erdoğan declares three-month state of emergency," *The Guardian*, 21 July 2016, www.theguardian.com/world/2016/jul/20/erdogan-bans-academics-from-travel-holds-first-post-coup-security-meeting-ankara-turkey [accessed 7 October 2017].

4   Middle East Institute, "Turkey's relations with the E.U., MEI VantagePoint," filmed 1 June 2017, Youtube video, 19:54, published 6 June 2017, www.youtube.com/watch?v=ZhmnQ1YHau4 [accessed 5 November 2017].

5   Middle East Monitor, "German troops to leave Turkey's Incirlik base in July," Middle East Monitor, 18 June 2017, www.middleeastmonitor.com/20170618-german-troops-to-leave-turkeys-incirlik-base-in-july/ [accessed 26 July 2017].

5

The Brexit shock

> To be sure, some individual Continentals could be brilliant and sometimes admirable, but most of them were bizarre, slippery, and often incomprehensible. They ate inedible things such as octopuses, frogs, and snails. "Only foreigners waltz backward," Englishmen said contemptuously in the past, when the waltz was still fashionable
>
> Luigi Barzini, *The Europeans*[1]

The British attitude toward "the Continent," captured above, that kept the UK for many years from applying for membership in the European Community, may sound anachronistic today. The English are surely less contemptuous of their European neighbors than they were when Italian journalist Luigi Barzini in 1983 colorfully characterized their view of the continentals. But are they? The 2016 referendum forcing the UK to begin negotiations to leave the European Union – a process known as "Brexit" – suggests that many Brits still see a wide cultural, political and economic channel between themselves and "the Europeans."

The 2016 referendum favoring by a close margin British departure from the European Union was a shock to British politics and to the European Union. But it also created uncertainties affecting transatlantic relations, international affairs and the future of the West more generally. As the first of two 2016 quakes that rattled the West, Brexit reflected perhaps the growing power of populist sentiment and rejection of globalism and distance regulation/governance. Brexit turned out to be a warning that neither traditional assumptions nor professional opinion polls could be completely trusted in this new era. Applauded by Vladimir Putin, neo-nationalist and populist politicians in Europe, including France's Marine Le Pen, as well as by US presidential candidate Donald Trump, the outcome raised questions about how the overall strength and importance of the EU would be affected and whether Britain's role in the world would be diminished. While Brexit's story will play out over several years, its implications for transatlantic relations could be substantial, particularly considering the other developments discussed in these pages.

Expectations and surprises

On Thursday, 23 June 2016, millions of British voters went to the polls to determine whether the United Kingdom was to remain a member of the European Union. Most opponents and proponents of departing the EU were led by opinion polls to believe that leaving would be rejected. Pollsters across the board, from *Huffington Post* pollsters to a YouGov poll conducted on election day, overwhelmingly predicted that "Remain" would triumph over the xenophobic, anti-immigration Vote Leave campaign. These projections, reassuring to most believers in liberal democracy and Britain's role in Europe, constituted, as the *New York Times* claimed, "yet another failure" in the realm of election prediction.[2]

Confident forecasts of a victory for Remain went out the window as the results flowed in during the early morning hours of 24 June. By only 3.78 percent – just over one million votes – Leave had won. What voters thought they knew as they went to the polls was turned upside down. Not only were projections across the board wrong, but the gravity of this surprise outcome also left a large part of the British political class dumbfounded. Across the English Channel and across the Atlantic, committed liberal democratic supporters and European Union fans watched in awe as Prime Minister David Cameron resigned his post to Theresa May, who promised to spearhead British departure from the EU. Brexit, as the decision came to be colloquially called, was the vote heard around the world.

Half-hearted European convictions

This story did not start in 2016, and should be understood as part of the long history of British early refusal to join in the European unification process, rejection by French president Charles de Gaulle of the UK's credentials when London did first apply, and eventual joining with exceptions to protect the UK's view of its own sovereignty, national identity and world role.

The Western alliance that took shape after World War II was handicapped by the British refusal to become more closely involved in post-war continental European affairs. The United Kingdom had been centrally involved in shaping the Western alliance and had promised to maintain forces on the Continent, at least so long as the troop presence in Europe did not conflict with British global commitments. But the British commitment to Europe was highly qualified and purposefully distant. The United Kingdom could not see itself as any part of a European unity movement. Its European role in the 1950s was, in effect, an extension of its special relationship with the United States and a distraction from British global political and military involvements. Furthermore, British foreign trade with the Commonwealth remained more substantial than that with continental Europe.

In the 1960s, a new generation of British politicians decided the United Kingdom should join the European Economic Community, but the commitment to Europe remained highly qualified. As a result, Britain's first tentative approach to Europe in 1963 ran into General de Gaulle's veto. De Gaulle accurately perceived Great Britain's commitment to Europe as still prejudiced by its Commonwealth ties and, most important, by its special relationship with the United States. He saw Great Britain as an "Atlanticist" Trojan horse. It is not hard to imagine de Gaulle proclaiming today: "*Je te l'avais dit. La Grande-Bretagne rest perfide Albion.*" [Translation: "I told you so. Great Britain never stopped being *perfidious Albion.*"]

In 1967, de Gaulle vetoed the UK's second application for membership. By the time Britain made its third attempt to join the Community, much had changed. De Gaulle had been replaced by Gaullist president Georges Pompidou, whose prestige was not at issue over British membership in the European Community. Along with changes on the Continent, British circumstances had substantially altered. British defense policy had become more Eurocentric with the withdrawal of its forces east of Suez. British trade with the Commonwealth had declined in the 1960s as a share of total British foreign trade, while commerce with continental Europe had steadily increased. The special relationship with the United States had become less and less of an equal partnership, as symbolized by the British withdrawal from a far-flung global presence. Great Britain became a member of the EEC on 1 January 1973.

The English, as a people, still had not fully accepted their place as a "European" country. Even today, some Brits still talk of "going to Europe" when they cross the English Channel. But by the early 1970s, it was already more than clear to objective observers that Britain's strategic interests could be served most effectively as a European, regional rather than global, power.

The debate over England's place in Europe, however, extended well into the next century, keeping open questions about the future of the European project – questions that seemed to be answered by Brexit. The factors that led to the fateful referendum built on the foundation of Euroscepticism that had colored British attitudes to the continent since the end of World War II. But new elements had entered the picture as well.

The UK: not all-in with the EU

The European Community that the UK had joined in 1973 became the European Union in 1991, following the end of the Cold War. In 1985, five EC countries had signed the Schengen

Agreement, creating a borderless area among them. In subsequent years, more countries joined and, by 2017, twenty-six of the twenty-eight EU members had abolished passport and border controls at their shared borders. But the UK and Ireland never joined the Schengen zone. When the 1993 Treaty of Maastricht called for creation of a monetary union – the Eurozone – the UK did not join.

Despite these important exceptions qualifying the UK's membership in the EU, the British remained seriously divided over their future in this project. On one side were the traditional sceptics who believed that membership in the EU robbed the UK of precious sovereignty, even with the exceptions. They saw their case as increasingly justified by ineffective EU responses to the great recession and emerging immigration issues, including its terrorism component. On the other side, generally younger, more cosmopolitan Brits were increasingly committed to membership in the EU and the attendant opportunities that they saw for their future. As one expert put it, "Brexit has pitted younger, more affluent, and cosmopolitan urban Britons against the older, poorer, and less educated ones in the rural and postindustrial parts of the country."[3] This British division looks remarkably like similar divisions on the Continent and in the United States. On both sides of the Atlantic, extreme right populist tendencies and parties have been energized by voters who "are angry at their financial instability, stagnant or declining living standards, and loss of jobs to emerging economies. And they have blamed it on the migrants arriving on their shores."[4]

Party politics

The case against the EU was brought largely by the United Kingdom Independence Party (UKIP). Prominent Eurosceptic politician and controversial commentator Nigel Farage took over leadership of UKIP in 2006 as the party had already begun realizing significant electoral growth based largely on its anti-EU, anti-immigrant platform. Farage aligned with Donald Trump, played on anti-Muslim themes to hype concern about terrorism and presented distorted perspectives on the economic dangers of immigration. UKIP became the leading British PRR party, pressuring the governing Conservatives on both EU and immigration issues. UKIP's populist rhetoric and right-wing themes capitalized on fears and concerns of voters – some legitimate and some exaggerated – about immigration, terrorism and intrusions in their lives from a distant EU decision-making center in Brussels.

In 2015, Conservative prime minister David Cameron promised to unite his party and went on to win a majority over all other parties in the House of Commons, the first Conservative leader in twenty-three years to do so. Cameron had promised an "in–out" referendum in 2013 to counter UKIP's threat to the Conservative base. After the 2015 success, Cameron presumably did not need to follow through with the referendum. But the Conservative victory did not relieve pressure to negotiate a "better deal" with the EU. While Cameron attempted to negotiate with Brussels, EU members and leaders rejected the idea of adjusting EU rules for the UK. Germany's Angela Merkel, dealing with migrant issues of her own, particularly opposed Cameron's asking for a British exception to the EU freedom to live and work anywhere inside the EU. As Cameron soon discovered, immigration would become the basis of the UKIP-led Vote Leave campaign, deploying fear tactics and promulgating false "facts" to fuel Euroscepticism.

Cameron's position was complicated by the fact that he had made enemies across the aisle, most notably Gordon Brown, the Labour prime minister who Cameron displaced in 2010. When presented with the opportunity to reach across the aisle, Jeremy Corbyn, who had become leader of the Labour Party in opposition, supported the case against Brexit, but with little conviction or enthusiasm. Even Gordon Brown pleaded with Corbyn to oppose Brexit more actively, but he demurred. Meanwhile, Cameron's more conservative colleagues, Boris Johnson and Michael Gove, fed the Vote Leave fires, dividing the Conservatives' parliamentary party and isolating Cameron.

Economic considerations faced off against sovereignty concerns in the "Brexit" campaign. Claims by the Remain campaign that leaving the EU would devastate the British economy were countered by Eurosceptic arguments that progressive EU economic integration would lead to a Brussels-dominated "superstate" controlling British lives and qualifying the UK's sovereignty. They also argued that leaving the EU would enable the UK to exploit worldwide trading opportunities and vastly increase GDP – claims not supported by most objective experts. Vote Leavers drew on the words of the late Conservative icon Margaret Thatcher, who had asserted in 1988 that "We have not successfully rolled back the frontiers of the state in Britain, only to see them re-imposed at a European level with a European super-state exercising new dominance from Brussels."[5] Calls for de-regulation spread like wildfire among "Thatcherite" Tories.

In the months leading up to Brexit, the debate intensified, pitting moderates against radicals. Days before the referendum, Prime Minister David Cameron stood in front of No. 10 Downing Street, making his final pitch against Brexit. "Brits don't quit," he pleaded, asking viewers to consider their children and grandchildren.[6] While Cameron visibly struggled to make the Remain case, some Conservatives claimed that he was in a trap of his own making. Cameron was haunted by the fact that the participation of John Major's former Conservative government in the European Exchange Rate Mechanism ended disastrously after just two years. After Major's resignation in 1997, Cameron re-established party power by promising to "resist further European integration," which eventually led to his 2013 offer to hold a referendum on EU membership. He obviously hoped to appease Eurosceptic arguments through the offer of a referendum, believing that it would surely fail. But Cameron's strategy backfired, and both Cameron and the Remain campaign fell victim to the populist-led fear campaign against EU membership – a campaign aided and abetted by many of Cameron's fellow Conservative Party members.

Cameron was replaced as Conservative Party leader and prime minister by Theresa May, who in March 2017 initiated the process of negotiating the UK's departure from the EU. The process, under Article 50 of the Lisbon Treaty on European Union, promised to stretch out over many months or even years. Whether it will end up as a "soft" departure, with generous terms for the UK, or a more punitive approach, remains to be seen. There are pressures on EU members to ensure a healthy relationship with the UK, even as a non-member. But there are countervailing pressures as well. If it is too easy and beneficial for the UK to leave, other wavering EU member states might be tempted to escape as well. Already the term "Brexit" has been joined by Frexit, Öxit, Grexit, Departugal, Begum, Itleave, Nethermind, and other fun names to characterize possible EU exits. None of these has so far demonstrated any serious chance of succeeding. The risk of France leaving, for example, was demolished when pro-EU centrist Emmanuel Macron soundly defeated the extreme-right populist and EU-sceptic Marine le Pen for the French presidency.

Consequences

The Brexit vote to leave the EU is one of the most important victories yet for illiberal political movements in Europe – if one accepts that the UK is part of Europe, despite the beliefs of some Brits to the contrary. While the UK's leading populist radical right party – UKIP – did not win control or even direct participation in government, it nonetheless scared the hell out of the Conservatives and led them down the road to a disastrous consequence, and Cameron to political oblivion. It had a major impact on the UK's future financial, economic and political health as well as its international commitments and influence. It could have serious consequences for British and European security as well as for the transatlantic alliance.

It is virtually impossible to predict with any certainty how British exit from the EU will affect the UK's future economic and financial interests. Much depends on the deal that is negotiated with the EU. The initial judgment of financial markets was that

Brexit would leave the UK weaker, as the pound fell to a thirty-year low. It recovered slightly but then hit some turbulence again in reaction to the snap election that Prime Minister May called in June 2017 (in which her Conservative Party lost its parliamentary majority). In the longer run, the pound may face more pressure. As the Brexit negotiations proceed, financial markets will react to the attendant uncertainty surrounding Britain's economic and financial future, perhaps constraining foreign investment. Another variable is the choice made by Scotland, where the referendum favored staying in the EU. The decision to leave revived the internal Scottish debate on seeking independence, which had lost in a referendum in 2014. But the results of the June 2017 parliamentary vote saw Scottish nationalists, led by Nicola Sturgeon, lose twenty-one seats, suggesting that Sottish voters were not as supportive of independence from the UK as some had thought.

While the generosity of the deal with the EU may be the most important variable, there are a few others as well. The UK will need to ensure not only that it will have access to EU markets, but also that it can maintain access to non-EU markets. At the July 2017 G20 summit, May generally focused in her bilateral discussions on building rapport with countries outside of the EU, hopeful about future trade agreements. President Trump, for his part, supported May's goal, alluding to the special US–UK relationship and claiming that he and Prime Minister May had been working on a trade deal that would be "a very, very big deal, a very powerful deal, great for both countries."[7] Trump emphasized that, with the new trade deal, the UK will thrive outside of the EU.

In addition, May used the gathering to talk trade with Japanese prime minister Shinzo Abe, making clear that an EU–Japan trade deal should be accompanied by a parallel UK–Japan deal post-Brexit accord. Despite May's optimism, there is no guarantee that post-Brexit trade deals will come easily, and a good chance they will come at a serious cost to the UK as well as May's political standing.

The UK's financial and economic future will also depend on

how successful May's government is in pursuing its agenda of freeing up enterprise inside the UK, avoiding the creation of new obstacles to innovation and growth when replacing EU regulations. One of the most difficult challenges will be deciding how open post-Brexit Britain will be to immigration. Despite the rhetoric from the far right that helped pass the Brexit referendum, the UK has greatly benefited over the years from immigrants adding their skills to the British economy. One source of Brexit collateral damage could be to deny access to talented citizens of EU member states and even to force many European residents in the UK to return to their home countries. If the UK does not manage to solve this problem, it could suffer significant long-term economic losses in addition to the human cost of disrupting so many lives.

President Barack Obama's administration had preferred that the UK remain in the EU. It fit with the Obama desire for the EU to take on a larger international leadership role as well as with the fact that the UK traditionally carried a transatlantic perspective into EU councils. Donald Trump, as a candidate for the presidency, had aligned with the Leave campaign. In fact, the leader of the UK's populist radical right party – UKIP – Nigel Farage, was a strong supporter of Trump. This aside, the conservative agendas of President Trump and Theresa May could be used to their mutual advantage.

The "special relationship" between Great Britain and the United States has a long and deep history. During a 1946 lecture tour of the United States, Winston Churchill traveled to tiny Fulton, Missouri, where, in one speech,[8] he coined the term "special relationship," articulating the unique US–UK bond. Until now, Churchill's "ardent Atlanticism" has been sustained by governments of all parties in London and Washington. During the Brexit process, when British relations with the Continent may at times be testy, London needs a strong working relationship with the United States. Whether President Trump and Prime Minister May can sustain healthy transatlantic ties remains to be seen. They both have issues with some EU members, and perhaps that will incline them to lend mutual support. They share an ideological distrust of EU bureaucrats and promised their electorates that they would renegotiate trade deals, reviving mercantilist notions versus free trade agreements, and refusing to recognize economic benefits of immigration.

British departure from the EU, on balance, would be a net loss for the EU. The UK has frequently been a drag on some of the more integrative approaches favored by continental EU members. But it has brought British common sense, practical solutions, and Atlanticist and global perspectives to the table that have made the EU a more formidable union. This is to say nothing of the fact that a significant part of the EU's economic and financial strength will no longer be under the EU's collective roof. In 2015, the UK's share of the EU's Gross Domestic Product was 17.5 percent, second only to Germany among EU members. The UK's contribution to the EU budget in that year was over 15 percent of the total. Whether the loss of that contribution will be compensated by increased contributions by the remaining members or a reduction in expenditures is already being debated inside the EU. Moreover, the EU post-Brexit will simply not swing as much economic weight as before. The departure will increase Germany's relative economic power and political influence, even though neither Germany nor its partners are comfortable with growing German heft in the organization.

In terms of strategic military impact, the fact that the UK will remain a leading member of NATO will take some of the sting out of the impact of Brexit on European security. However, to the extent that the EU aspires to develop independent military cooperation on the European level – something old that has been made new again by Donald Trump's unreliable leadership of the alliance – the British departure will handicap any future efforts in this direction. This prospect could be mitigated should the UK and the EU negotiate a post-Brexit bilateral defense cooperation agreement, but it will be hard to compensate fully for the absence of British capabilities, leadership and perspectives in the EU mix.

The bottom line is that Brexit will weaken the EU in many ways. As one commentator observed in the wake of the referendum, "Brexit will harm the EU's cohesion, confidence and international reputation. The biggest consequence of all, therefore, is that Brexit will undermine the liberal political and economic order for which Britain, the EU and their allies and friends around the world stand."[9]

Brexit, without question, weakens the West. The UK, in leaving the EU, is not leaving the West. It will not necessarily adopt illiberal policies because it is no longer a member of the pro-Western EU club. But weakening the EU amounts to weakening the West. It is a gift to Russia's president Putin, who favors and promotes anything that divides or takes away from the West's key institutions: NATO and the EU. And this blow to the West was followed in 2016 by the Trump political tsunami in the United States. It is to this storm across the Atlantic that we turn next.

Notes

1   Luigi Barzini, *The Europeans* (New York: Simon & Schuster, 1983), 59.

2   Nate Cohn, "Why the surprise over 'Brexit'? Don't blame the polls," *New York Times*, 24 June 2016. www.nytimes.com/2016/06/25/upshot/why-the-surprise-over-brexit-dont-blame-the-polls.html [accessed 7 October 2017].

3   Jonathan Hopkin, "Brexit backlash: the populist rage fueling the referendum," *Foreign Affairs*, 21 June 2016, www.foreignaffairs.com/articles/united-kingdom/2016–06–21/brexit-backlash [accessed 21 August 2017].

4   Ibid.

5   Margaret Thatcher, "Speech to the College of Europe ('The Bruges Speech')," Margaret Thatcher Foundation, 20 September 1988, www.margaretthatcher.org/document/107332 [accessed 6 October 2017].

6   Michael Holden, "'Brits don't quit', Cameron declares as EU referendum in balance," *Reuters*, 20 June 2016. www.reuters.com/article/us-britain-eu/brits-dont-quit-cameron-declares-as-

eu-referendum-in-balance-idUSKCN0Z6199   [accessed   7 October 2017].

7 Jack Sommers, "Donald Trump's vision of a post-Brexit trade deal could be very bad for Britain," *Huffington Post UK*, 12 August 2017, www.huffingtonpost.co.uk/entry/brexit-trade-deal-us-uk_uk_598b2bfce4b0d793738c0284 [accessed 7 October 2017].

8 Winston Churchill, "Sinews of peace," *History Guide*, 5 March 1946, www.historyguide.org/europe/churchill.html [accessed 7 October 2017].

9 Tony Barber, "Five consequences of the UK's exit from the EU," *Financial Times*, 24 June 2016. www.ft.com/content/b1a2d66e-3715–11e6–9a05–82a9b15a8ee7 [accessed 23 July 2017].

6

The Trump tsunami*

"I alone can fix it."
Donald J. Trump, accepting Republican nomination
for President of the United States[1]

The second major 2016 shock for transatlantic relations came in the United States with the Republican nomination and then electoral victory of Donald Trump – someone who had self-identified as both a Democrat and Republican over the years and donated money to candidates of both parties. Trump raised concerns throughout the campaign as someone who played on the fears of Americans concerning both terrorism and their own financial well-being, blaming not only the administration in power but also the system of government and international commitments for which he claimed the Obama administration and the Democratic Party stood. This quintessential populist campaign had much in common with the approaches of European populist radical right parties.

Candidate Trump blamed "bad" international trade deals for the loss of manufacturing jobs in the United States. His style and approach ran roughshod over the more traditional Republicans against whom he contended the primaries, and then turned enough swing states in the general election to win the presidency, despite receiving close to three million fewer votes than his opponent, Hillary Clinton.

During the campaign, Trump displayed his disdain for the European Union and for NATO as well, calling the transatlantic alliance "obsolete" and claiming that low levels of European defense spending meant that the Europeans had not been "paying their dues." In one stunning attack on NATO, he suggested that the United States should not be willing to come to the defense of an ally that had not been spending enough on defense – this despite the collective defense commitment (Article 5) of the 1949 North Atlantic Treaty, a commitment that every American president since 1949 has unconditionally reaffirmed.[2] In office, Trump moderated some of his statements on NATO and the EU, perhaps influenced by the more traditional people he chose as his Secretary of Defense, retired General James Mattis, and his second choice of national security advisor, General H. R. McMaster (still on active duty). In June 2017, and again in a 6 July speech in Warsaw, Poland, Trump asserted that he did in fact intend to honor NATO's collective defense provision.[3] But occasional presidential tweets and public statements suggested that his basic attitudes had changed little, as he continued to argue that the European allies "owed" money to the alliance and to the United States.

If Brexit was a shock for transatlantic relations, the election of Trump was a tsunami, arguably jeopardizing nearly seventy years of transatlantic commitments, political assumptions and security cooperation. It also gave rise to speculation in Europe about the possibility of an independent German nuclear deterrent, or an EU one, and renewed talk of a "European army," all not necessarily more likely despite the uncertainties created by President Trump.

Candidate Trump rejected most trade arrangements made in recent years or anticipated in the future as "unfair" to the United States and "bad deals," including the North American Free Trade Agreement (NAFTA), which he vowed to renegotiate, and the Trans-Pacific Partnership, from which he withdrew the United States after becoming president. Negotiations for a potential free trade accord between the United States and Europe – the Transatlantic Trade and Investment Partnership – were put in limbo. But it was his attitude toward NATO that most directly assaulted the values and interests that define the West.

NATO is a unique alliance in world history, outlasting its original purpose of deterring the Soviet Union and, in so doing, demonstrating the persistence of the shared values and interests among its members. Donald Trump is a disruptive president, rejecting past practice, procedures and principles. The interaction between NATO and this president in just a few months upended decades-old assumptions about the transatlantic alliance and the presidency.

Trump psychology

When one examines President Trump's approach to almost any policy issue, including alliance relations, it is useful to consider the psychological profile that apparently lies behind virtually every policy utterance, speech or, yes, tweet on the subject. This president appears to be motivated by a variety of factors, including the instincts born of a narcissistic personality, his need to be praised, his personal family and financial motivations, and his admiration for "strong" leaders.

Aspirants to higher office seldom achieve their goals without elevated levels of self-confidence, and American politicians get elected in part by being loved, or at least respected. President Trump's behavior, however, has differed sufficiently from that of any predecessor to entice professional, as well as amateur, psychologists into the public dialogue. Critical assessments have ranged from a "diagnosis" of a narcissistic personality disorder to simply not being an empathetic person. It is also clear that Trump's career as a wealth-endowed investor with several children intimately involved in his business world (and then to some extent in his public service role) influences his decision-making framework. His admiration for "strong" leaders, irrespective of their policies or human rights records, apparently was a product of his experience in the business world – uninformed by standard diplomatic procedure, "presidential" norms or even American values.

One reason that analysts and commentators have looked

for almost any explanation of Trump's positions and behaviors is that he doesn't appear to have come to office with any clear or consistent political ideology. Historically, Trump has bounced back and forth between declared affinity for the Democratic and Republican parties.

We will not look here for an ideological or even policy-based explanation for Donald Trump's approach to the North Atlantic Treaty Organization and its members, or to Western values in general. Rather, this chapter traces the evolution of Trump's approach from his candidacy for the Republican nomination, to the election campaign, and finally during his first year as president.

Historical perspective

Before surveying the contemporary record, a brief comparative historical note may be in order. Throughout the nearly seven decades since NATO's founding, US participation in the alliance reflected the fact that the Congress, and particularly the Senate, considered itself a joint manager with the executive branch of the "transatlantic bargain." From the very beginning, the congressional partner regularly raised questions about the persistent burden-sharing issue. This questioning began with the initial debate in the Senate on whether it should give its advice and consent to the Treaty. The administration of President Harry Truman reassured Senators that the European allies would contribute to their own defense and that the United States would not end up carrying a disproportionate share of the burden.

As the European states recovered from the devastation of World War II, some Senators argued that the Europeans had become capable of defending themselves. Montana's Senator Mike Mansfield famously promoted resolutions from the mid 1960s into the early 1970s that sought to force administrations to begin withdrawing US forces from Europe. While US administrations – Democratic and Republican – sought ways to contain the financial burdens and to get the Europeans to compensate the United States for some of NATO's costs, the established pattern persisted into the post-Cold War years. Over all these years, the Congress did most of the complaining while successive presidents of both parties urged allies to do more but largely defended the alliance and its costs as necessary for US national interests.

In this area, Trump has already reversed institutional roles with his burden-sharing complaints and his threats to abandon key commitments in the 1949 Treaty. The Congress, in response, has largely assumed the role of NATO-defender, giving strong bipartisan support (the Senate voting 98–2) to a further expansion of the alliance to include the small Balkan state of Montenegro, with some members expressing concern about the new Russian threat to Europe, and wondering why President Trump was not nearly as concerned. Later, by the same tally, the Senate voted to impose new sanctions on Russia and to require President Trump to get congressional approval before easing current sanctions on Russia.

Candidate Trump and NATO

Candidate Trump's critique of NATO, and US allies in general, did not come totally out of the blue in the primary campaign. Before that time, there is very little on the public record documenting Trump's views on NATO, but he did make one major dive into the burden-sharing issue when, in 1987, he was considering a run for the presidency. Trump ran an "open letter" in several major newspapers "on why America should stop paying to defend countries that can afford to defend themselves."[4]

During the campaign, Trump's first major statement on the alliance came in a March 2016 interview with the *Washington Post*.[5] In response to a question, Trump called NATO "a good thing," and said he did not want the United States to "pull out." He then went on to suggest that the United States was taking virtually all the burden of responding to Russia's aggression against Ukraine when it was US allies whose security was more affected. The entirety of his NATO comments was set in the framework that also was driving his positions on trade: "the world is taking advantage of the United States, Uncle Sam has been both overly generous and stupid, we are not as wealthy as we once were, and we need to change all of that."

In some ways, Trump's going-in position was not that different from Barack Obama's complaint that there were too many "free riders" among America's allies,[6] or the lecture by Robert Gates when he was leaving his position as Secretary of Defense that the maldistribution of burdens in NATO could undermine the US commitment to the alliance.[7]

It could be said, therefore, that there is a broad American consensus that the allies should "do more." However, while the Obama and Gates perspectives reflected considerable thought, research and experience, Trump's betrayed a very superficial knowledge of NATO, its founding Treaty, its history, and realities of international and transatlantic relations. The position comes from his largely profit-oriented, transactional point of view that underlies the "America First" appeal to his base of support.

The next development of the Trump position came just days later, when Trump described NATO as "obsolete."[8] Trump explained, "NATO was set up a long time ago — many, many years ago when things were different. ... We were a rich nation then. We had nothing but money. We had nothing but power." At first blush, this statement seemed to transform Trump's burden-sharing complaint into a generalization that "NATO is obsolete." However, on Twitter the following day, he clarified the reason for his statement, tweeting "N.A.T.O is obsolete and must be changed to additionally focus on terrorism as well as some of the things it is currently focused on!"[9] This suggested that his problem with NATO was not only that it costs the United States too much and the allies are not paying their "fair share," but also that NATO is neglecting his top priority: fighting terrorism in general and ISIL in particular.

In June 2016, when NATO announced it was creating the new post of Assistant Secretary General for Intelligence, intended to improve coordination of intelligence assessment on Russia as well as on the Middle East and terrorism, Trump claimed that the change had come in response to his complaints.[10] In fact, a NATO official confirmed the alliance had been planning to create this post "for some time" before Trump's criticism.[11]

Of course, Trump's terrorism complaint – the foundation for his "obsolete" generalization – totally ignored the fact that NATO had taken on the most demanding active combat mission in its history following 9/11, volunteering to command the International Security Assistance Force in Afghanistan to which NATO allies and partners contributed thousands of troops to fight al Qaeda and the Taliban.

The list of other NATO activities related to fighting terrorism includes the 2008 establishment of the NATO Cooperative Cyber Defence Centre of Excellence in Tallinn, Estonia. The primary motivation for the center was provided by the Russian cyber threat to NATO ally Estonia, but its mission became even more important as ISIL improved its ability to use cyber weapons and social media against the West.

In other words, while Trump may have been right that NATO could expand its work against terrorism, the alliance was already headed in that direction. His assertions may have added urgency to the process, but they also revealed his ahistorical and superficial understanding of the alliance.

The terrorism-based charge of NATO's obsolescence also ultimately provided another demonstration of Trump's narcissistic personality. When NATO secretary general Jens Stoltenberg visited the White House in April 2017, President Trump bragged that he no longer considered NATO obsolete because the alliance had taken his criticism to heart. In his joint press conference with Stoltenberg, Trump said, "I complained about [what NATO can do to fight terrorism] a long time ago, and they made a change and now they do fight terrorism. I said it was obsolete. It's no longer obsolete."[12] What a transformation.

On 27 April 2016, the third leg of candidate Trump's NATO stool appeared almost as a logical progression following his charges of inadequate allied defense spending and lack of counterterrorism efforts. In a major foreign policy speech to the Center for the National Interest, in which Trump laid out his "America First" theme, he suggested that he would reverse nearly seventy years of US policy toward its NATO Treaty commitment. He declared: "The countries we are defending must pay for the cost of this defense, and if not, the U.S. must be prepared to let these countries defend themselves. We have no choice."[13]

Trump's statement suggested that for allies not paying their "fair share" of NATO expenses the United States should reconsider its North Atlantic Treaty commitment to come to their defense if they were attacked. NATO's 1949 charter does not specify exactly what each ally will contribute to the alliance. The Treaty's Article 3 suggests simply, "the Parties, separately and jointly, by means of continuous and effective self-help and mutual aid, will maintain and develop their individual and collective capacity to resist armed attack." But alliance members have all pledged (in Article 5) that they will regard an attack on any ally as an attack on themselves. This "mutual defense commitment" is the heart of the alliance. It has been invoked only once: when the NATO allies agreed to regard the 9/11 attacks on the United States as an attack on all of them, and offered assistance to their North American ally.

No US administration, Republican or Democratic, has ever called NATO's mutual defense commitment into question. If President Trump were to make this part of his administration's foreign policy, it would almost certainly force allies to decide what they would need to do to account for a much less reliable American ally. The prospects for an autonomous European defense system had already potentially lost a key player with the British decision to leave the European Union. But even before Trump's November 2016 victory, speculation started building about the possibility for an autonomous European nuclear deterrent, an independent German nuclear weapons program and European accommodation of Russian interests.

President Trump

After the elections, the European allies were largely left to see what the new administration would bring to the table, in terms of policies and people in key positions.

US allies were somewhat relieved when President Trump did not initially repeat the threat to abandon the US collective defense commitment even though he did not abandon demands for more allied defense spending. When Trump nominated retired general James Mattis as secretary of defense, the allies interpreted the selection as a possible sign of a return to orthodoxy. But Trump's obvious inclination to "do a deal" with Russian president Putin and his nomination of Exxon CEO Rex Tillerson – who had received Russia's Order of Friendship – as secretary of state strengthened speculation that Trump might direct Tillerson to negotiate a deal, perhaps removing the sanctions imposed on Russia for its 2014 aggression against Ukraine, including annexation of The Crimea.

On his inaugural visit to NATO headquarters, Secretary Mattis delivered a hybrid model of Trump's NATO policy. Mattis essentially said that the allies must increase defense spending and that failure to do so could have consequences. At a Brussels press conference on 15 February, Mattis said, "America will meet its responsibilities, but if your nations do not want to see America moderate its commitment to the alliance, each of your capitals needs to show its support for our common defense."[14] The Mattis message reaffirmed President Trump's words on allied defense spending and cloaked his threat concerning the US commitment to collective defense in words that sounded more like Robert Gates's 2011 warning.

Prior to the Mattis visit to Brussels, Trump had met with British prime minister Theresa May. The two appeared to hit it off, and May even said that Trump had given "strong support" to NATO. Candidate Trump had endorsed the UK's departure from the EU, which British voters had favored narrowly in a June 2016 referendum, and May was now intent on carrying out that mandate. That, combined with the UK's position as one of the few NATO countries that was already meeting NATO's agreed 2014 goal of spending at least 2 percent of GDP on defense by 2024, had set up the two leaders for a successful meeting.

The same could not be said of the circumstances surrounding Trump's first meeting with German chancellor Angela Merkel. As the leader of the EU's political and economic powerhouse, Merkel also represented one of the leading "free riders" on American defense efforts, at least from Trump's point of view. The Trump–Merkel discussion on 17 March concluded with a press conference that put the awkward relationship on full view. After avoiding the traditional handshake with Merkel in the Oval Office photo opportunity, Trump declared in the press conference: "I reiterated to Chancellor Merkel my strong support for NATO as well as the need for our NATO allies to pay their fair share for the cost of defense. Many nations owe vast sums of money from past years, and it is very unfair to the United States. These nations must pay what they owe."[15]

The suggestion that Germany and other allies owed past dues to the alliance, or even to the United States, reflected once again Trump's lack of understanding of how NATO works, or even for what the alliance stands. Allies do not contribute to the alliance by paying dues, other than providing their share of funds to support common programs like NATO infrastructure, including NATO headquarters in Brussels. The main "contribution" made by each ally is the money spent on their own defense efforts. There is no question that many allies have not spent as much on defense since the end of the Cold War, or even throughout the history of the alliance, as the United States would have liked. But the notion of allies owing "past dues" is completely inconsistent with the terms of the North Atlantic Treaty and the allies' practice over the last seventy years.

Despite the facts of the situation, President Trump persisted, tweeting on 18 March, after Merkel had headed back to Berlin, that Germany must pay "vast sums of money to NATO & the United States" for the "powerful, and very expensive, defense it provides to Germany!"[16]

Finally, Trump's attitude toward NATO cannot be divorced

from his peculiar perspective on Russia and its president, Vladimir Putin. Trump had studiously avoided critiquing either Russia or President Putin. That fact, combined with the on-going investigations of links between the Trump campaign and Russia's clandestine efforts to influence the outcome of the US elections in Trump's favor, has cast a continuing cloud over Trump's approach to NATO. How can allies put their trust in an American president who seems conflicted about one of the most important threats to many NATO nations and to Western interests and values more generally?

Against this backdrop, a NATO summit meeting was scheduled for 24–25 May 2017, as a highlight of Trump's first international trip as president, in which he was scheduled to visit Saudi Arabia, Israel, Vatican City, Brussels (for the NATO summit) and Taormina, Italy (for the 43rd G7 summit). The NATO allies were collectively holding their breath in expectation of more Trump bombast. But Trump's new national security advisor, the well-respected general H. R. McMaster, who had replaced discredited Trump nominee retired general Michael Flynn, offered reassurance. Prior to Trump's departure from Washington, McMaster said: "President Trump understands that America first does not mean America alone. ... To the contrary, prioritizing American interests means strengthening alliances and partnerships that help us extend our influence and improve the security of the American people."[17]

The most important test of Trump's approach to NATO came on 25 May during the Brussels gathering of alliance leaders. The meeting was technically built around formal dedication of NATO's shiny new headquarters, but the new facility played second fiddle to the Trump display of America first-ism.

As the date for President Donald Trump's arrival in Brussels neared, Trump's White House remained upside down with controversy while, in Brussels, allies worried about how to deal with the unpredictable yet demanding American president. The controversies swirled around issues of interest to NATO – charges of Trump collusion with Russia to affect the presidential election and a Trump dump of classified information into the laps of

Russian foreign minister Sergei Lavrov and Russia's reputed spymaster ambassador to the United States, Sergey Kislyak.

By the time Trump arrived in Brussels, internal consultations among the allies and with Secretary General Jens Stoltenberg had produced a strategy designed to please the American president while defending against his possible assaults on the alliance and individual allies. The strategy included limiting the time available for formal presentations (to avoid boring Trump) and not preparing a final "declaration" to avoid potential battles over contentious issues, like burden-sharing and Russia relations.

The visit to NATO headquarters began with dedication of displays at the entrance intended to commemorate the fall of the Berlin Wall and the 9/11 attacks on the United States. In Trump's remarks, after asking for a moment of silence for the victims of the terrorist attack in Manchester, England earlier in the week, and condemning terrorists, he lit into a critique of defense spending levels of NATO members. His burden-sharing remarks did not come as a surprise, as they reflected his previous positions. The big question was whether President Trump would clarify his position on the American commitment to collective defense. According to press reports, "Mr. Trump offered a vague promise to 'never forsake the friends that stood by our side' in the aftermath of the Sept. 11 attacks — a pledge that White House officials later said amounted to an affirmation of mutual defense."[18] This was hardly the ringing endorsement for which the European allies had hoped.

The weak affirmation of collective defense was made even more telling by the fact that, once again, Trump chose not to challenge Russia on its aggression against Ukraine and threats to NATO allies. He focused instead almost entirely on the terrorism and refugee issues. As if to add an exclamation mark to his hard line on underperforming allies, he at one point pushed his way to the front of the gathering of leaders, physically brushing aside Dusko Markovic, the prime minister of Montenegro, scheduled to become NATO's newest member on 5 June 2017. The great irony, or the explanation, if one is inclined toward conspiratorial thinking, for the rude behavior (replayed all over social media) was that Markovic had led his country through a successful bid to join NATO in the face of strong overt and clandestine Russian opposition.

Before Trump left Brussels, the alliance announced that NATO, as an organization, would formally join the anti-ISIL coalition (all members were already contributing to the effort in one form or another). To demonstrate that they were listening to Trump's burden-sharing complaints, the allies agreed to develop annual national plans for how they intend to meet the 2014 defense investment pledge, covering cash, capabilities and contributions.

More trouble ahead ...

With the summit in the rearview mirror, more turmoil lay ahead, for the alliance as well as for President Trump. The most important consequence of the summit and the G7 meeting that followed was the reaction of German chancellor Angela Merkel to her interactions with Trump. In a campaign appearance after the meetings, Merkel said the days when Europe could rely on others was "over to a certain extent."[19] Merkel's comment, made in the context of the British exit from the EU, Trump's demands on NATO and his calling German automakers "very bad," suggests that Trump handed Vladimir Putin an important victory in his campaign to split the Western alliance.

Trump's participation in NATO's "mini-summit" may eventually be interpreted as an important way station on his learning tour of NATO issues. But it remains to be seen whether the president wants to learn anything that would conflict with his well-established bias and, if he does, whether he will make a good student. The bad news for Atlanticists is that his management of the alliance could last a full four, or even eight, years. Over time, breaking with time-tested US policy toward NATO and the West could leave America not "first" but alone, by critically damaging the trust and mutual confidence that have made the transatlantic relationship work.

Ironically, within weeks Trump was headed to Europe again, this time for a summit of the G20, a gathering of the world's leading economic powers, including a much-anticipated (or dreaded, depending on one's perspective) bilateral meeting with Russia's Putin. On his way to the summit in Hamburg, Germany, hosted by Chancellor Angela Merkel, the White House scheduled a stop in Warsaw, Poland, for the president to make a major speech before a very friendly audience. The Warsaw visit was hosted by the Polish government led by Trump's soul-mate populist radical right party, Law and Justice, which bussed in enthusiastic supporters from outside Warsaw.

Trump's speech, delivered in front of the historic Uprising Monument at Krasinski Square, praised the Polish people's sense of nation and courage to defend it against a long history of assaults.[20] Trump made a clear assertion of America's support for NATO collective defense: "I would point out that the United States has demonstrated not merely with words but with its actions that we stand firmly behind Article 5, the mutual defense commitment." At the same time, he bragged inaccurately that it was his insistence that had produced increases in NATO defense spending (increases that had long been planned following Russia's aggression against Ukraine). In addition, he claimed to be supporting "Western values" and said that they were strengthened by "the bonds of culture, faith and tradition that make us who we are" and weakened by "the steady creep of government bureaucracy." This sounded to some more like his political platform than the openness and inclusivity that most see as hallmarks of liberal democracy. Trump's hosts enjoyed virtually everything about his well-crafted speech because it played to much of the political philosophy shared by Trump and the Law and Justice Party.

Trump moved on to a less welcoming reception in Hamburg, where thousands were waiting to protest not just Trump but what they saw as the wealth and control represented by the G20. In Hamburg, Trump found himself on the outside looking in on issues of climate change and multilateral trade issues, as the other Western leaders had pretty much decided to move on without the usual US lead. Trump's focus was far more on his meeting with Putin than with leaders of allied countries. The meeting stretched on for over two hours, and produced a partial ceasefire agreement in Syria. US officials after the meeting claimed that Trump had raised the issue of Russian meddling in the US elections, and that the two leaders had agreed to disagree. The Russian side, however, suggested that Trump had accepted Putin's denial of culpability – a denial that ran counter to what the entire US intelligence community had long-since concluded.

It was subsequently revealed that Trump also met with Putin for a post-dinner conversation that lasted as long as one hour. There was no American record of the meeting (other than Trump's recollection that it was just an exchange of "pleasantries" and discussion of Moscow's ban on American adoptions of Russian children) because the only other person in the discussion was Putin's interpreter; there was no American one – thought by most to be a significant diplomatic and national security mistake.

While Trump was busy pleasing the Poles and pandering to Putin, the reins of Western leadership were slipping out of US hands. This could be seen not only in the convergence of non-US Western views on trade and the environment, but also on the future leadership of the West.

Is the US abdicating leadership of the West?

President Donald Trump is widely seen in Europe and by his numerous critics in the United States as having abdicated American leadership of the West. When German chancellor Angela Merkel traveled to Washington in March 2016 to visit Trump, one headline blared "The Leader of the Free World Meets Donald Trump."[21] This perception of abdication was based partly on Trump's persistent refusal to criticize Vladimir Putin for his kleptocratic foreign policy, annexation of Crimea and aggression against Ukraine. It was solidified by Trump's meetings with NATO and G7 leaders in Europe in late May and then additionally confirmed when Trump announced he would pull the United States out of the Paris climate agreement (which incidentally gave China the opportunity to claim that it was now the "responsible" international leader on climate issues). The question then became whether Merkel's Germany would be able to provide the leadership that the West and its predominant institutions – NATO and the European Union – need. The answer, most likely, is no.

The peculiar thing about leadership is that, to be effective, the leader must have followers who believe following is in their own interest. Leadership is not bestowed automatically, particularly among nation states. To get loyal followers, the leader must choose paths followers are willing and able to travel.

The United States has provided such leadership most of the time since World War II. The fact that the United States was the leader of "the West" was unchallenged, even if the quality of that leadership was frequently questioned, for example during the Vietnam War and, more recently, in response to the US invasion of Iraq. But there was no country that could challenge American leadership of NATO (even though France on occasion tried).

US support for the European integration process and the reassurance provided against external threats and internal imbalances enhanced America's leadership role. Many smaller European states remained wary of Germany becoming too strong again, distrusted a France that spoke of European unity but often on its own terms and questioned Great Britain's commitment to the European project. US involvement in Europe, from the founding of NATO in 1949 until the Trump presidency, provided a crucial and stable foundation for the process of community-building to move forward, even at times of serious transatlantic discord. No one European power would dominate on the continent, in part because of the way the European Union was designed and in part because of benign American power in the background.

As we know, there is no such formal position as "the leader of the free world," or of "the West," and it is an open question whether any other country has the inclination, respect, resources and capabilities to take on the responsibilities that go with the honorific. But, with the American president seemingly abdicating his responsibilities, the leading candidate would seem to be Germany, as led by Angela Merkel.

Germany's economic strength has made it the economic and financial leader of the European Union. But the main reason to look to Germany is that Merkel's politics are most clearly rooted in the principles and priorities that define "the West." Those values are articulated in the 1949 NATO Treaty, whose preamble asserts that the allies share a belief in individual liberty, democracy and the rule of law. In recent years, major NATO statements have added "human rights" to the list. The European Union, of course, endorses a similar set of values.

The problem is that leadership of the West in a conflicted regional and global environment requires something else: power. In this area, Germany comes up short. This is an intentional consequence of history. After World War II, France and other European states hoped to ensure that Germany could not become a threat to peace for a third time in the same century. The United States wanted to make sure that Germany's potential could eventually be included in a defense against the Soviet Union, but agreed that limits should be placed on Germany's offensive and particularly its nuclear weapons potential. Perhaps even more important, Germany's post-war leaders and all German governments since have worked hard to establish a new national ethos: Germany would no longer be a warrior state.

Nevertheless, throughout the Cold War, Germany provided substantial forces on NATO's front lines facing the East. In the almost three decades since the disintegration of the Soviet Union and the Warsaw Pact, Germany and other allies have relaxed their military efforts. Trump has taken Germany to task for only spending around 1.2 percent of its GDP on defense, and reports abound of equipment shortages and readiness issues in the Bundeswehr. Perhaps of greater concern is the fact that, even though German public opinion strongly supports NATO, it is skeptical about coming to the support of an ally under attack, perhaps in part because Germans don't want to send troops on another American mission like Afghanistan.

Today, the lessons of the twentieth century remain firmly planted in the German polity. That contributes to American frustration with Germans being unenthusiastic about additional military spending or sending their troops into combat.

One of the early German reactions to Donald Trump's assaults on the NATO allies was speculation about Germany becoming a nuclear weapons state. Suggestions that Germany should "think the previously unthinkable," raised by a prominent German newspaper and a conservative member of the German parliament, were met with cautionary responses and alternative proposals.[22] One proposal envisioned creating a European deterrent on French and British nuclear capabilities, with Germany funding the operation. But neither an autonomous German nuclear force nor a European deterrent force are near-term prospects. They are simply too potentially destabilizing in the former case (as well as a breach of the Nuclear Non-Proliferation Treaty) and most likely, in the latter, a bridge too far beyond sovereign control of nuclear weapons for France and the United Kingdom.

In some respects, Trump may have succeeded beyond his wildest imagination in his Europe/NATO policies. He boasts he has made our European allies do things that no other American president has done. And, to be honest, he has helped unite the Europeans. Unfortunately, he has largely united them against the United States, rather than behind it. The result may include more European spending on defense, but a much less cooperative transatlantic relationship, which could be disastrous for US efforts to gain international support for its policies. Would America's European allies volunteer to invoke Article 5, as they did on 9/11, in response to a future terrorist attack if Trump's policies undercut trust in and sympathy for the United States?

The Trump impact on transatlantic relations has also given new life to proposals for intensified European defense cooperation. The European allies certainly could do more for their own defense, and part of this could come from concerting efforts, reducing duplication, sharing missions and other practical cooperative steps. But an effective European alternative to NATO would likely cost far more than what they are currently able to produce for their contributions to NATO. This is to say nothing of the new complications resulting from the British decision to leave the European Union. Some might see this British move as facilitating EU military cooperation, but it takes more away in potential capabilities than it adds in the ease of making political decisions.

This suggests that, in the near term, NATO will remain the preferred option for all European members of the alliance. It would take a complete and total American departure from the alliance to change this outlook. And, despite the many uninformed and careless comments uttered by the American president, the United States is nonetheless increasing its contributions to defense in Europe, and particularly deployments in the north and east intended to deter any Russian intrusions, whether by massive force or Little Green Men.

This story seems to me like the initial large boom that usually opens a fireworks show: you know there is a lot more to come, including presumably a dramatic finale. The level of uncertainty is enhanced by the fact that, although Trump has won a four-year term as president, the various investigations of his campaign and administration's connections to Russia raise questions about whether he will serve the entire term, to say nothing of winning a second one.

Meanwhile, the first months of the Trump presidency produced a dramatic shift in global opinion of the United States. According to the well-respected Pew survey published in June 2017, "The sharp decline in how much global publics trust the US president on the world stage is especially pronounced among some of America's closest allies in Europe and Asia, as well as neighboring Mexico and Canada. Across the 37 nations polled, Trump gets higher marks than Obama in only two countries: Russia and Israel."[23]

It is ironic that President Trump has assaulted the closest American allies while saying virtually nothing critical about America's leading geopolitical adversary: Russia. On balance, it must be said that Donald Trump has thus far in his term done more to weaken American leadership of the West and to put American interests at grave risk than even his most severe critics might have anticipated before his inauguration.

Uncertainty reigns on the European side as well. Angela Merkel has firmly established her claim on at least the moral leadership of the West, to add to Germany's more comprehensive leadership of the European Union. Merkel's criticism of Trump will do her no harm at home, as few Americans are less popular in Germany than Donald Trump.

As has been the case in Europe for over six decades, the French–German couple plays an important role in European and transatlantic affairs. When the French electorate stood up to both established left, right and far-right parties and elected Emmanuel Macron as president, Merkel and Germany gained an important ally. Macron still faces challenges in his own country. But he and Merkel seem to believe that they are riding a new tide that rejects extreme nativist populism, and that forms a solid platform from which they can reject Donald Trump's American extremism.

Macron in fact demonstrated his adept leadership by inviting Trump to help commemorate Bastille Day, France's independence celebration. The visit went well, and marked a bit of a diplomatic triumph for Macron. But Trump had to return to Washington to face the continuing investigation into his campaign's relationship to Russian meddling and hacking in the 2016 elections.

Against this backdrop, the transatlantic crystal ball remains clouded. The United States currently can lay no claim to leadership of the West, or even of the transatlantic alliance, as the positions and posturing of Donald Trump have at least temporarily relinquished that responsibility. At the same time, Germany and Angela Merkel occupy the moral high ground, but are not able to check off all the requirements for the task of comprehensive Western leadership. President Macron can claim a victory at home, and his alliance with Germany adds some stability to the European side of the alliance. The United Kingdom, led by

Prime Minister Theresa May, is now and will continue to be distracted by the challenge of managing an ill-considered departure from the European Union that seems likely to make her country weaker and less influential.

To the extent it is possible to predict, the absence of good alternatives suggests that when the fireworks show comes to its finale, NATO will remain standing and the United States will once again lay claim to leadership of the West. This will not likely come during the presidency of Donald Trump, but could come from his successor, whether a Democrat or Republican. One of the remarkable products of the Trump disruption is a convergence, at least in the Congress, of the two parties in support of NATO and Western values. This could suggest that the Western alliance might emerge from the current crisis even stronger. But the question will be how much damage to mutual trust and confidence will be incurred in the meantime. On the current path, transatlantic relations are headed toward a dialogue based on mutually shared mistrust, creating opportunities for Russian president Vladimir Putin to exploit.

Moving on ...

We now have examined how illiberalism on both sides of the Atlantic, Turkey's progression away from Western values, the UK's projected exit from the EU and Donald Trump's shock to the Western system have proven traumatic not only for the transatlantic relationship but also for the West in general. The next chapter looks at how Western values and institutions that so many believe in might be saved and reinvigorated.

Notes

*   This chapter is based in part on analysis originally presented in: Stanley R. Sloan, "Policy series: Donald Trump and NATO: historic alliance meets a-historic president," H-Diplo International

Security Studies Forum, 8 June 2017, https://issforum.org/roundtables/policy/1-5am-nato [accessed 8 October 2017].

1 Yoni Applebaum, "'I alone can fix it'," *The Atlantic*, 21 July 2016, www.theatlantic.com/politics/archive/2016/07/trump-rnc-speech-alone-fix-it/492557/ [accessed 6 October 2017].

2 Krishnadev Calamur, "NATO schmato?" *The Atlantic*, 21 July 2016, www.theatlantic.com/news/archive/2016/07/trump-nato/492341/ [accessed 3 November 2017].

3 David Frum, "The falsehood at the core of Trump's Warsaw speech," *The Atlantic*, 7 July 2017, www.theatlantic.com/international/archive/2017/07/trump-warsaw-speech/532917/ [accessed 8 October 2017].

4 Ilan Ben-Meir, "That time Trump spent nearly $100,000 on an ad criticizing U.S. foreign policy in 1987," *BuzzFeed News*, 10 July 2015, www.buzzfeed.com/ilanbenmeir/that-time-trump-spent-nearly-100000-on-an-ad-criticizing-us?utm_term=.lkZD MGNZE8#.enr7j8l9V6 [accessed 8 October 2017].

5 Post Opinion Staff, "A transcript of Donald Trump's meeting with the Washington Post editorial board," *Washington Post*, 21 March 2016, www.washingtonpost.com/blogs/post-partisan/wp/2016/03/21/a-transcript-of-donald-trumps-meeting-with-the-washington-post-editorial-board/?tid=ss_tw&utm_term=.e6f28 e21f4b3 [accessed 8 October 2017].

6 Mark Landler, "Obama criticizes the 'free riders' among America's allies," *New York Times*, 10 March 2016, www.nytimes.com/2016/03/10/world/middleeast/obama-criticizes-the-free-riders-among-americas-allies.html?_r=0 [accessed 8 October 2017].

7 Thom Shanker, "Defense Secretary warns NATO of 'dim future'," *New York Times*, 10 June 2011, www.nytimes.com/2011/06/11/world/europe/11gates.html [accessed 8 October 2017].

8 "Complete Donald Trump interview: NATO, nukes, Muslim world, and Clinton," *Bloomberg Politics*, 23 March 2016, www.bloomberg.com/politics/videos/2016-03-23/complete-trump-interview-nato-nukes-muslims-and-hillary [accessed 8 October 2017].

9 Donald J. Trump, "N.A.T.O. is obsolete....", *Twitter*, 24

March   2017.   https://twitter.com/realDonaldTrump/status/
712969068396093440 [accessed 3 November 2017].

10 Louis Jacobson, "Donald Trump mischaracterizes NATO
change and his role in it," *Politifact.com*, 16 August 2016, www.
politifact.com/truth-o-meter/statements/2016/aug/16/dona
ld-trump/donald-trump-mischaracterizes-nato-change-and-his-/
[accessed 3 November 2017].

11 Louis Nelson, "NATO: Trump had nothing to do with intel
post," *Politico*, 8 June 2016, www.politico.com/story/2016/06/
donald-trump-nato-intelligence-post-224081   [accessed   8
October 2017].

12 Kevin Liptak and Dan Merica, "Trump says NATO no longer
'obsolete'," *CNN*, 12 April 2017, www.cnn.com/2017/04/12/
politics/donald-trump-jens-stoltenberg-nato/   [accessed   8
October 2017].

13 Donald J. Trump, "Trump on foreign policy," *National Interest*,
27 April 2016, http://nationalinterest.org/feature/trump-foreign
-policy-15960 [accessed 8 October 2017].

14 Dan Lamothe and Michael Birnbaum, "Defense Secretary
Mattis issues new ultimatum to NATO allies on defense spending," *Washington Post*, 15 February 2017, www.washingtonpost.
com/news/checkpoint/wp/2017/02/15/mattis-trumps-defense-
secretary-issues-ultimatum-to-nato-allies-on-defense-spending/
?utm_term=.268c36fd75b5 [accessed 8 October 2017].

15 Jeff Mason and Andreas Rinke, "In first Trump–Merkel meeting, awkward body language and a quip," *Reuters*, 17 March
2017,   www.reuters.com/article/us-usa-trump-germany-idUSK
BN16O0FM [accessed 8 October 2017].

16 Donald J. Trump, "...vast sums of money....", *Twitter*, 18
March   2017,   https://twitter.com/realDonaldTrump/status/
843090516283723776 [accessed 3 November 2017].

17 Quoted in Noah Bierman, "Trump prepares for first overseas
trip, with anti-globalism at bay," *Los Angeles Times*, 15 May
2017, www.latimes.com/politics/la-na-pol-trump-globalist-2017
0515-story.html [accessed 8 October 2017].

18 Michael D. Shear, Mark Landler and James Kantermay, "In
NATO speech, Trump is vague about mutual defense pledge,"

New York Times, 25 May 2017, www.nytimes.com/2017/05/25/world/europe/donald-trump-eu-nato.html?hp&action=click&pgtype=Homepage&clickSource=story-heading&module=first-column-region&region=top-news&WT.nav=top-news [accessed 8 October 2017].

19 Quoted in Henry Farrell, "Thanks to Trump, Germany says it can't rely on the United States. What does that mean?" *Washington Post*, 28 May 2017, www.washingtonpost.com/news/monkey-cage/wp/2017/05/28/thanks-to-trump-germany-says-it-cant-rely-on-america-what-does-that-mean/?utm_term=.def364cdb312 [accessed 8 October 2017].

20 Donald J. Trump, "Remarks by President Trump to the people of Poland | July 6, 2017," *The White House*, 6 July 2017. www.whitehouse.gov/the-press-office/2017/07/06/remarks-president-trump-people-poland-july-6-2017 [accessed 8 October 2017].

21 James P. Rubin, "The leader of the free world meets Donald Trump," *Politico.com*, 16 March 2017, www.politico.com/magazine/story/2017/03/the-leader-of-the-free-world-meets-donald-trump-214924 [accessed 8 October 2017].

22 *The Economist*, "Germans are debating getting their own nuclear weapon," 4 March 2017, www.economist.com/news/europe/21717981-donald-trumps-questioning-natos-credibility-has-berlin-thinking-unthinkable-germans-are [accessed 8 October 2017].

23 Richard Wike, Bruce Stokes, Jacob Poushter and Janell Fetterolf, "U.S. image suffers as publics around world question Trump's leadership," Pew Research Center, 26 June 2017, www.pewglobal.org/2017/06/26/u-s-image-suffers-as-publics-around-world-question-trumps-leadership/ [accessed 16 August 2017].

7

Has illiberalism brought the West to the brink of collapse? Can the Western system be reinvigorated?

Many forms of Government have been tried, and will be tried in this world of sin and woe. No one pretends that democracy is perfect or all-wise. Indeed it has been said that democracy is the worst form of Government except for all those other forms that have been tried from time to time.

Winston Churchill, House of Commons, 11 November 1947.[1]

No. Illiberalism has not yet brought the West to the brink of collapse. But the populist radical right surge that has hit both sides of the Atlantic in recent years has revealed failures of and weaknesses in Western democracy that, if not attended to, could destroy the unity of principles and purpose that have defined "the West" for over seven decades.

Following the violent and deadly white supremacist march in Charlottesville, Virginia, in August 2017, conservative Republican US senator Orrin Hatch tweeted: "We should call evil by its name. My brother didn't give his life fighting Hitler for Nazi ideas to go unchallenged here at home."[2] But, as we have seen, the far right is challenging liberal democracy on both sides of the Atlantic, aided and abetted by elected officials and foreign enemies.

The previous chapters suggest that the nations of "the West" have assumed for over seven decades that liberal democracy, based on individual liberty and the rule of law, was not only the most effective system for governing, but was also the most moral, measured by religious or purely humanistic standards. The leading enemy of such standards in the first half of the twentieth century had been Germany's "national socialism," a Nazi regime led by the brutal dictator Adolf Hitler whose policies brought the Holocaust and whose aggression led to the Second World War.

After the Western powers had won that war, a new challenger emerged: the communist regime in the Soviet Union. Until the Warsaw Pact – the Soviets' Eastern European alliance – started crumbling in 1989, followed by the disintegration of the Soviet Union, the West fought a Cold War against this antagonistic world power and its system of government that denied what Western governments thought were basic human rights. The United States wisely – generously and in its own self-interest – initiated the Marshall Plan to help rebuild European nations devastated by the war and to give democratic governments a chance to survive in the recovery period. The Marshall Plan's requirement that the European recipients organize to use the aid most effectively helped start the process of community-building that led to today's European Union. Wise Europeans and Americans created the North Atlantic Treaty Organization to defend Western values and interests from external threats.

At the end of the Cold War, Western countries breathed a sigh of relief. Some observers, most notably Francis Fukuyama in *The End of History and the Last Man*, suggested that liberal democracy had finally demonstrated that it was the inevitable wave of the future, capable of withstanding all future threats.[3] But new challenges soon replaced such optimism.

No single event or political, economic or military development was responsible for what happened over the next three decades. The September 11, 2001 terrorist attack on the United States led to wars in Afghanistan and Iraq – wars that would not go away even when some thought they had been "won." Part of the failure of Western powers was to believe that their political system could be forcefully transplanted into countries whose existing systems had been banished but which had no historical experience with or traditions of democracy. The conflicts, which became part and parcel of a war on terrorism, drained the West not only of resources but also of confidence in the future. The Arab Spring gave reason for optimism concerning the overthrow of autocratic regimes in the Middle East. But the optimism was short-lived as, in most cases, more liberal structures failed to take root.

The Great Recession of 2007–8, caused by the collapse of a speculative bubble, had already undermined optimism in the future. When recoveries were mounted by Western countries, the benefits largely flowed to the already wealthy, rather than to average citizens. In the United States, this supported populist movements on both the left and the right. On the left, "Occupy Wall Street" emerged to protest big capital and financial institutions whose excesses had sparked the recession. Vermont's Senator Bernie Sanders emerged to lead the populist protest of the concentration of wealth in "1 percent" of the population and to campaign for the Democratic presidential nomination. But the malaise also created openings for parties and movements on the far right that were not committed to the values and political systems of the West. Those movements were aided and abetted by Russia's Vladimir Putin, who was determined to try to re-establish Russia as a major power, and even to retrieve regions lost when the Soviet Union disbanded. In addition to strengthening his own illiberal, autocratic regime in Russia, Putin initiated both overt and covert efforts to support radical right parties and regimes throughout the West, and to support the election of Donald Trump in the United States.

In a short period of time – two traumatic years – the optimism that had blossomed at the end of the Cold War was slipping away. The question now is whether this drift will lead to a disaster for the idea and institutions of the West.

Even though today's circumstances are unique, the challenge to liberal democracy is not, as the history of the twentieth century made clear. Sir Michael Howard, the distinguished British military historian, posed what he called "the liberal dilemma"[4] in 1977. Defending Western values, according to Sir Michael, may require the use of force against external threats, but more importantly requires non-military actions to deal with internal challenges.

How can we best defend liberal Western democracies against today's threats? Western nations deploy military capabilities to deter external threats and to defend the country if deterrence fails.. As a rule, internal enemies of liberal democratic systems cannot be defeated by military force, particularly when they use the openness of the system to attack it. Defense against internal threats usually requires that believers in liberal democracy and its values attend to the issues that are giving rise to support for less liberal approaches. On the international level, the goal of nations joining together to defend against an illiberal and threatening regime, like the Soviet Union, for example, depended primarily on military deployments and strategies. However, that defense can come into conflict with the desire to maintain liberal democratic systems in charge of the allied states. This has not always been possible, as noted in the first chapter. NATO tolerated an undemocratic regime in Portugal and military juntas in Greece and Turkey, judging that it was more important to maintain a united front against the Soviet threat than to maintain internal liberal democratic purity.

Today, the challenge is to do both: improve the West's democratic systems and institutions to diminish the internal dissatisfaction that can give rise to illiberal tendencies supported by populist movements, while providing sufficiently strong defenses against external threats – in the contemporary period against both Russia and Islamist terrorism. The two tasks in many ways have become thoroughly interactive. Russia seeks to use the West's open democratic systems to influence electoral outcomes to favor its interests while ISIL and similar groups use the freedoms presented by liberal democratic systems to engage in attacks against those systems. As retired general David Petraeus testified before the US House Armed Services Committee in February 2017, "President Putin ... understands that, while conventional aggression may occasionally enable Russia to grab a bit of land on its periphery, the real center of gravity is the political will of major democratic powers to defend Euro-Atlantic institutions like NATO and the EU."[5]

The first step toward dealing with these challenges is to develop a clear analysis of the factors that have created opportunities for external and internal enemies of the West. We have volunteered some perspectives in the preceding chapters. The next step is to identify the changes (reforms) to the Western political, economic and financial systems to address these issues. The final step is to take political action to demonstrate that the political center in Europe and in the United States has the ideas and the capacity for breaking ideological and policy deadlocks to respond to popular concerns and needs. Supporters of liberal democracy will also have to demonstrate that the institutions of the West – most importantly the European Union and NATO – are serving the needs not only of governments, elites, the financial world and big business, but also those of average citizens.

While failure to deal successfully with the challenges to Western values could have a devastating impact on security cooperation among NATO and EU states, most of the necessary steps are not to be found in the realm of security policy, but rather must emerge from political, economic and financial system reforms. If these reforms can be successful, popular support for defense spending and measures to strengthen counterterrorism will come as a derivative product, as people will see that "the West" and its values are worth defending.

Perhaps this falls into the category of "easier said than done." But the potential cost of failure could be regression into some sort of contemporary "dark ages" dominated by authoritarian regimes supported by the wealthiest individuals and corporate interests, in which Putinism could become the rule rather than the exception.

A radical centrist populist strategy

The logical recommendation that emerges from this analysis of what constitutes and threatens "the West" is a strategy that could be called "radical centrist populism." In Western democracies, most outcomes that benefit the populace and are consistent with liberal democratic values are best shaped and implemented around the center of the political spectrum. The process almost always requires compromise among contending ideas and political interests, but it does not need to be a "status quo" outcome. In fact, the threats and challenges described in this volume suggest that radically different policies from those currently dominating governance approaches in Western nations may be required to preserve the West and the application of its values. In some Western political systems – the US one, for example – it would be radical simply for the two major parties to work toward bipartisan solutions to the nation's problems.

This discussion closes with suggestions about how a radical centrist populist Western strategy could be applied to deal with the threats and challenges discussed earlier, reinvigorating the Western system (see Box 1).

ISIL and terrorism

The West has little choice but to support the fight against radical Islamist terrorist groups like ISIL and al Qaeda, deploying Western military capabilities where necessary. However, while Western nations must take steps to protect themselves, they need to avoid "owning" the fight against the terrorists. The fight on the ground needs to be based largely on forces from Muslim countries, with the support of Western military capabilities when necessary. In the long run, the most basic need is for Muslim states to resolve the conflict within their ranks over how to confront modernity and to what extent the Islamic world believes that theological politics is compatible with representative government. Moderate Islamist parties have been successful in Tunisia and Morocco, suggesting a possible model. As Janet Breslin-Smith argues (see Chapter 2), Western nations need to push Muslim states to confront the dilemmas to which faith as a political tool gives rise in the contemporary world, and to close ranks against brutal dictatorships in their ranks – with

Box 1. What do we mean by "radical centrist populism"?

Radical: Because the goal is to move decisively away from today's highly partisan conflicted politics and to be willing to consider creative and even revolutionary ideas from the left or right if they will benefit the people and are consistent with liberal democracy. A great historical example of radical centrist populism is the Marshall Plan assistance program, discussed earlier.

Centrist: Because it is in the political center that liberal democracies find pragmatic agreements that move countries ahead. The willingness of political factions to compromise across party lines is key to progress in liberal democracies.

Populism: Because governance in liberal democracies is ultimately about participation in the democratic process, seeking outcomes that benefit the people, and therefore the nation, is critical. Not everyone can be pleased with everything, but if substantial groups are left behind, liberal democracy is not working sufficiently well to deny political credibility to illiberal options.

Syria's Assad regime at the head of the list. Those that fail to do so, or that feed the fires of radical Islam, should be confronted and not coddled – as has happened with the West's treatment of some Middle Eastern Arab states, including Saudi Arabia, with tolerance based largely on dependence on their importance as oil suppliers. Such confrontations can be more private than public, but should remind Arab leaders that tolerance of support for radical Islamist movements and parties is inconsistent with a close partnership with the United States and other Western countries.

As with most problems, the West must also heal its own self to deal with the Islamist terrorist threat. Western states need more effectively to provide opportunities for Muslim minorities to integrate into their societies and political systems. This is one area in which many other Western states could learn from the Canadian example as well as the American one which, at least until Trump, has been relatively welcoming and integrative. Governments should take radical practical steps to deal with unemployment among Muslim youth through ambitious educational and training programs that reduce the tendency for the hopelessness and dead-ender mentalities that can lead young Muslims off to volunteer for ISIL and other terrorist organizations. While poverty and marginalization are not the only factors in the radicalism of Muslim youth, they do play a significant role. Radical centrist populists should promote creative and constructive approaches to these factors as important tools for reducing the future threat of Islamist terrorism.

Russia

In the long run, it is not wrong to hope and even work for a relationship with Russia that affords the country and its people a respectable and productive place in the international system. However, so long as Russia is controlled by a political system based on one dominant, corrupt leader – Vladimir Putin, or those who might succeed him – with only the trappings of democracy and little respect for individual liberty or the rule of law, it is hard to imagine that the West will have such an opportunity. This suggests that the West will have little choice but to maintain sufficient military capabilities to deter Russia from believing that its interests would be served by either outright military aggression or subtle subversive attempts to weaken Western democracies.

In terms of military deterrence, it is critically important for the United States to remain actively involved in NATO's defenses against Russian threats. No American president should ever again threaten to remove the US commitment to NATO collective defense and Article 5 of the North Atlantic Treaty. This commitment is much more than just a "gift" to the European allies. Rather, it underlines the important Western values that provide the foundation for everything that can be counted as a Western interest. Moreover, the United States is the only NATO member that has ever benefited from invocation of Article 5. Political cohesion and shared responsibilities remain core ingredients of a successful defense of the West, are frequently more important than specific military capabilities.

There are also steps that Europeans can take to maintain transatlantic values and cooperation while they are being questioned in Washington.

First, the NATO allies should demonstrate that they are actively supporting the pledge to spend at least 2 percent of their GDP on defense by 2024, with 20 percent of defense spending going to new equipment, research and development. What each country buys with its defense spending is critically important, but the process all starts with the input: as is often said, quantity has its own quality.

European NATO and EU nations should also look for opportunities to make no- and low-cost defense improvements, and to improve intra-European and transatlantic cooperative efforts, for example enhancing terror-related intelligence-sharing operations through Europol, internally and with partner nations. When improvements can be demonstrated, they should be publicized. Back in the waning years of the Cold War, the so-called "Eurogroup" served as a publicist in the United States for European defense efforts. Perhaps the European allies should revitalize the concept. The Europeans speaking in this way directly to American politicians, opinion leaders and, importantly, taxpayers, could provide a helping hand to American radical centrist populists who believe in reaffirming a strong US role in NATO.

Second, it is important for European countries to express appreciation for US contributions to their security. Americans know that the United States has not always made the best decisions when it has come to the use of force, but Europeans should recognize that their freedom and democracy have benefited greatly from the American role in European security. European expressions of this sentiment to American Members of Congress and the American public reinforce US support for continued transatlantic cooperation.

Third, as a means both of maintaining Western unity and keeping the door open for cooperation with Russia when it is in the West's interest, the United States, Canada and their European allies should continue to endorse a policy of "defense, deterrence and dialogue." This approach, built on NATO's diplomatic strategy given birth during the Cold War in the 1967 Harmel Report, remains a sensible and balanced approach to dealing with Russia. The United States and Russia share a joint responsibility for management of their strategic nuclear relationship. Irrespective of other issues in the relationship, strategic stability remains a shared US–Russian interest. The US secretary of defense and the Russian defense minister and senior military officers on both sides should be in routine contact to ensure that no misunderstandings lead to a possible nuclear exchange.

While the door is kept open to cooperation, it needs to be slammed shut on Russian attempts to undermine Western political systems using new cyber weapons to complement the old-fashioned means of covert operations.

How should the West respond to cyber-subversion? First, the United States must provide Western leadership to present a unified front against Putin's attempts to undermine Western democracy. So far, President Trump's approach to dealing with Russia and Putin has failed to reassure most Americans and allies that his administration has struck the right balance. The president's denial of the conclusion supported by the entire American intelligence community that Russia actively worked to ensure his election seriously weakens US leadership in this area and increases US vulnerability to future meddling. The only way out of this dilemma is for the American people and their representatives to insist that the Trump green light for Russian meddling is turned to a red light. Both parties in both houses of the US Congress in the summer of 2017 took a step in this direction by passing a strong set of sanctions against Russia with the provision that they could not be unilaterally overturned by the president. Sanctions remain an important source of pressure on Russia but will be effective only if the United States and its allies remain united in their application.

Sanctions are a tricky policy tool, as they usually incur costs for the sanctioning countries and their commercial interests as well as for innocent civilians in the target country. The United States and its allies will have to work closely to ensure that the multilateral sanctions regime is maintained so long as is necessitated by Russian behavior. Perhaps the most difficult issue will be Europe's continuing reliance on Russian energy sources – in some respects a more reliable source than the Middle East but carrying with it Russian political, economic and financial leverage. The challenge in this area will be managing the disparate dependency levels in ways that ensure a fair distribution of costs and burdens among Western states to ensure that Russia does not benefit from its illegal seizure of Crimea and its continuing military assaults on Ukraine's independence.

Illiberal tendencies in Europe

Populist radical right alternatives to Western liberal democracy will continue to be an element of the political reality for most European countries. In a few cases – in Germany and Spain, most notably – an illiberal history has left such a painful wound on the body politic that extreme temptations in that direction have but limited chances for getting traction. But in virtually all European countries, a combination of circumstances in recent years has increased support for parties, groups and leaders who argue the case for less liberal democracy and more autocratic governance. The Great Recession and the refugee crisis over the past decade created particularly fertile ground in Western Europe for those radical populists who were prepared to turn popular dissatisfaction into fear and political action. In the new democracies of Central and Eastern Europe, the failure of democratic forces to resolve all the issues that remained in the wake of the overthrow of the Cold War, Moscow-dominated communist regimes created room for illiberal parties to increase their popularity.

In many European states, the straw that broke the camel's back of support for liberal democracy ended up being the challenges around the refugees who streamed across the Mediterranean escaping war and dictatorships in north Africa and the Middle East. If the EU, NATO and the West more generally value human rights, they cannot afford to abandon these refugees, regardless of populist-incited paranoia. European governments must take a radical centrist populist approach to the refugee problem to deny political space to the extreme right. European democratic centrists need to support the idea of a unified, EU-wide approach that would benefit all member states, taking specific interests of each state into account; aid border nations; provide more opportunities for legal migration and safe crossings for refugees; and reinvigorate and reunite a divided EU. Much of the difficulty in resolving the refugee crisis comes from individual members' economic concerns, but analysis suggests that the EU could more sustainably host refugees when working as one unit than could individual states.[6] Moving forward, states should host refugees or, if unable, contribute fiscally to their workforce integration and general support.

The European project at its core provides a welcoming framework for such an effort. But now a new approach is needed to revitalize this core structure. Those European politicians who are inspired by the idea of radical centrist populism could focus on rebuilding the popular base for the European project. Centrist leaders could reach out to the countryside – where populist radical right movements tend to get significant support – with sensible and politically sensitive approaches to dealing with refugee and other issues that have in the past created support for the radical right. Outreach, including sympathetic media coverage, would seek not only to listen to the views of the locals, but also to explain the benefits of maintaining the Western system. Such a public campaign with a focus on the people could help turn the European project into a populist one. Centrist activists should develop such a "movement" in each EU member state modeled on French president Macron's successful En Marche! campaign, sharing radical centrist populist goals but tailored to the specific conditions of each individual country. Through such a coordinated effort, including active social media campaigns, radical centrist populism could move forward, diminishing support for illiberalism throughout the EU.

In our survey of populist radical right parties in Chapter 3, we observed that the most common response of centrist parties to populist radical right challenges has been co-optation: adopting some of the tactics and rhetoric of illiberalism to undercut the natural constituencies of the radical right populists. This approach has produced some electoral success for centrist parties, but it is risky. It tends to lend legitimacy to illiberal policies and makes it more difficult for co-opting parties to move back to more centrist positions following the voting in which it was deployed. A more successful strategy has been non-cooperation, practiced in Belgium, which has succeeded in keeping populist radical right tendencies from corrupting centrist parties. If non-cooperation became more common in European political culture, then the center would be able to develop distinctly democratic and Western solutions. Non-cooperation has the capacity to enable radical centrist populism.

Given that no European state has yet fully succumbed to the populist radical right extreme of installing an authoritarian regime – even though a few have been infected by illiberal temptations, with Hungary, Poland and Switzerland coming to mind – there are clear opportunities for radical centrist populism to assert itself. In the wake of the British decision to abandon its membership in the EU, there is a temptation on the Continent to conclude that, without a reluctant Great Britain to hold up progress, the process of integration can run full speed ahead. This most likely is a deceptive perception, as nationalism remains a powerful instinctive force on the Continent, not just across the English Channel. A radical centrist populist approach should respond effectively to the popular perception that life is increasingly dominated by undemocratic bureaucracies a long way from local communities and interests. Europe can be more united, but it needs to be a Europe that respects and draws strength from the diversity that is Europe.

Turkey

Turkey is not a European state, but it is a member of NATO and has for many years aspired to be recognized as more than just a European neighbor and an EU associate. Those aspirations have been turned upside down by recent history, which has seen Turkey under President Erdoğan take a path away from the values and systems that define a Western state and even to seem to shift allegiances away from its Western allies and toward Russia and some of Turkey's Muslim neighbors.

Turkey, once again, demonstrates the difficulty for the West of being true to liberal democratic values while tending to geostrategic necessities. As a Muslim-majority nation, Turkey's secular democracy had been a hopeful sign that liberal democracy might be setting a good example for other Muslim states that were emerging from various undemocratic political histories. That hope is now diminished.

The West's strategy now must be to encourage a turn by Turkey back toward liberal democracy while, at the same time, avoiding a complete break with this strategically important country. Russia has already solidified its position in the region with its support for Assad in Syria, and Turkey's move away from NATO and toward strategic cooperation with Russia would be a huge loss for Western security. It has been tempting for some Western observers to muse about how Turkey could be removed from NATO, even though there are no provisions in the North Atlantic Treaty for such a step.[7] Turkey's chances of joining the European Union were already slim to none, despite formal promises by the EU, and forcing Turkey out of NATO could set Turkey totally adrift and perhaps into the welcoming arms of Putin's Russia.

Western nations should therefore speak frankly to the Turkish government through diplomatic and military channels about the steps that would reassure the West about Turkey's future political directions. Germany, despite strained relations in 2017, may have the best chance of exerting constructive influence, given the extent to which Turkish enterprises depend on the German export market. The goal is to keep Turkey attached to the Western alliance while working to move the country back to a democratic path. This process may require some time and patience, but Turkey is too valuable a country to give up on.

Brexit

The Brexit referendum was the first big shock to the Western system of 2016. But it could pale in comparison to the pain and division that negotiating British departure from the EU could bring to both sides of the English Channel. The West would have been better served by the United Kingdom remaining a member of the European Union. Are there ways that this could still happen? Perhaps, but it would require a virtual revolution of radical centrist populists in the UK to turn this ship around. For now, the focus is on how the damage can best be limited.

The first requirement will be attitudes of goodwill on the part of the EU members and the UK. As one of the West's key institutions and defender of Western values, ensuring the European Union's future well-being should be a shared interest of all in the West. At the same time, a separation agreement that helps the UK recover from the divorce is equally in the interests of the West. Britain cannot afford to accept harsh financial and economic consequences, while the EU cannot afford to finance a totally "soft" landing for the UK. Perhaps if the UK is allowed to remain in the single market for a prolonged period, the shock of separation for both the UK and the EU can be mitigated, or even avoided. One can only wish the negotiators well.

It is a good thing that Brexit has no direct effect on the UK's membership in NATO. However, it does potentially undermine prospects for effective European defense cooperation, and therefore progress toward a more substantial European contribution to the Atlantic alliance. It will be critically important for a post-Brexit UK to strengthen its role in NATO – avoiding major cuts in British defense spending – while negotiating new bilateral defense cooperation agreements with the EU and its leading members.

From a North American perspective, it appears that British democracy, while not in danger, may well be in trouble. Just as the political center has fallen apart in the United States, the British center seems equally weak. The current Conservative government is carrying forward a policy that won approval due to a mistaken political judgment by the previous Conservative prime minister and a populist radical right campaign that raised fears sufficiently to produce a marginal victory for the "Leave" campaign.

The political field would seem to be open to advocates of rebuilding the center, defined by this book's description of radical centrist populism. The "Leave" campaign played on issues that are of legitimate concern for British voters, including those that have produced support for radical right populists on the Continent and in the United States. Traditionally, the Labour Party might be expected to, and logically could, become the UK's main proponent of radical centrist populism. But under its current leader, Jeremy Corbyn, it has been stranded out on the far left, as a critic of the EU and NATO, and therefore not a current candidate to assume leadership of radical centrist populism in British politics.

In terms of transatlantic and Western interests more broadly, the UK needs a radical centrist populist revolution of its own, just as does the United States.

Trumpism

Without a doubt, the most important threat to Western values and interests in recent years has come from the extreme-right populist candidate who became president of the United States. This suggests that radical centrist populism has work to do on the American side of the Atlantic. Ironically, even though Donald Trump ran at the head of an enthusiastic Republican ticket, he hardly represented traditional Republican values, but rather a set of non-values beyond advancing his own interests, including his financial interests and those of his family. He immediately abandoned any pretense of providing leadership for the West – an unofficial position that American presidents have claimed since World War II. Instead, he showed a puzzling respect for enemies of Western values and interests, most notably his enthusiastic endorsement of dictators, including Russia's Vladimir Putin. He also found support among the most radical and violent of

American right-wing groups, consistently failing to condemn them or refuse to accept their support, as most other Republican and Democratic politicians have done.

It is fortunate that, at this writing, the United States still has a democratic electoral process that can and must be protected from Russian intrusion and protected from far-right violence. Those who accept the need for a radical centrist populist movement in the United States should work with like-minded Europeans to re-establish mutual trust and confidence between the United States and the European Union. Radical centrists should support the positions of American officials and politicians – of both parties – that favor cooperation in NATO and collaboration with the EU to help defend against external and home-grown threats to the West.

The investigations of Russian aggression against the American political system, and its intent of helping Donald Trump get elected, may yield information that leads to an early conclusion of the Trump presidency, but that is by no means certain. Nor is it clear what policies Trump's immediate successor might take. The next reliable decision point, therefore, is the 2018 mid-term elections. In the primaries leading up to and in the November elections themselves, those Americans who believe in the need for a new radical centrist populism should support candidates that demonstrate their belief in Western values and are willing to seek solutions to major problems across party lines. If the Republican Party remains committed to the Trump presidency, GOP congressional and state-level candidates will have to consider a choice between reverting to traditional conservatism or moving toward the centrist approach recommended here. For their part, Democrats may wish to borrow ideas from their party's left – including reforms of the health care system and more equitable taxation policies – but should look for solutions that can be agreed with moderate Republicans in the center.

A key goal of those Americans who believe in Western values should be to protect freedom of the press. President Trump has continuously assaulted all press sources that do not support his goals and actions. The extensive leaking of information from inside the government in the early months of the Trump presidency suggests the level of concern inside the government for the health of American democracy. Yes, leaking classified information is a bad thing, and all administrations, Republican and Democratic, have railed against it, but have been unable to stop it completely. However, it would not be nearly so widespread if the president were acting less like a narcissistic autocrat and more like a true democrat.

In the end, the goal of American radical centrist populism should be to return the country to a position as the leading defender and practitioner of Western values. This can only happen if politicians and publics support bi-partisan solutions to issues as a way of rebuilding the political center. No other approach will serve the country as well.

Beyond the traumas

These are just some of the policy areas that must be addressed to ensure that the ideas and interests of a liberal democratic West are not only defended but are also reformed and reinforced. But ensuring the future of the Western system needs to start now, and should involve all those who believe that systems of governance based on democracy, individual liberty, human rights and the rule of law can best guarantee our future.

The goal of the radical centrist in all Western countries should be:

1. to deter, where possible, and fight where required, external threats to the Western community of nations; and
2. to reinvigorate liberal democracy with centrist approaches that are sufficiently radical to bring constructive change and pragmatically responsive solutions to the needs of average citizens.

This will require revitalization of the political center in the American and other Western democracies. Political extremes can fire up electorates, but the political center is where the hard work is done and results are produced. The US and European political centers must become positive forces for constructive change, and then demonstrate the will to make it happen. Atlanticists must act as "radical centrist populists of the West" – those who subscribe to Western values and cooperate to defend them.

If Winston Churchill were with us today, I'm sure he would confirm that this "imperfect" Western system is nonetheless better than any of the alternatives. It should be the mission of the radical centrist populists of the West to preserve and energize it for the benefit of future generations on both sides of the Atlantic, and wherever else people choose to be governed in a Western-style liberal democratic system.

Notes

1   Winston S. Churchill, "The worst form of government," *winston churchill.org*, 11 November 1947, www.winstonchurchill.org/resources/quotes/the-worst-form-of-government [accessed 3 November 2017].

2   Quoted in Brooke Seipel, "Hatch: My brother didn't die fighting Hitler for Nazis to go unchallenged today," *Thehill.com*, 12 August 2017, http://thehill.com/homenews/senate/346348-hatch-my-brother-didnt-die-fighting-hitler-for-nazis-to-go-unchallenged-today [accessed 8 October 2017].

3   Francis Fukuyama, *The End of History and the Last Man* (New York: Free Press, 1992).

4   Michael Howard, *War and the Liberal Conscience* (New Brunswick, NJ: Rutgers University Press, 1977).

5   Joe Gould, "Petraeus warns Congress on Russia, immigration order," *DefenseNews.com*, 1 February 2017, www.defensenews.com/congress/2017/02/01/petraeus-warns-congress-on-russia-immigration-order/ [accessed 8 October 2017].

6   Pierre Vimont, "Migration in Europe: bridging the solidarity gap," Carnegie Europe, 12 September 2016, http://carnegie

europe.eu/2016/09/12/migration-in-europe-bridging-solidari ty-gap-pub-64546 [accessed 3 November 2017].

7   Doug Bandow, "Toss Turkey out of NATO: U.S. doesn't need civilian dictatorship or military junta," *Forbes*, 27 July 2016, www.forbes.com/sites/dougbandow/2016/07/27/toss-turkey-out-of-nato-u-s-doesnt-need-civilian-dictatorship-or-military-jun ta/#3853a94bfa54 [accessed 3 November 2017].

Select bibliography

Akkerman, Tjitske (2012) "Comparing radical right parties in government: immigration and integration policies in nine countries (1996–2010)," *West European Politics*, 35:3, 511–29, doi:10.1080/01402382.2012.665738.

Akyol, Kursat (2016) "15 years of Turkey's AKP: is it a success story?" *Al-Monitor*, 31 August, www.al-monitor.com/pulse/originals/2016/08/turkey-economy-heading-to-turbulent-times.html. Accessed 26 July 2017.

Arzheimer, Kai (2015) "The AfD: finally a successful right-wing populist Eurosceptic party for Germany?" *West European Politics*, 38:3, 28 January, 535–56, doi: 10.1080/01402382.2015.1004230.

Ashbee, Edward (2017) *The Trump Revolt*, Manchester: Manchester University Press.

Asthana, Anushka (2017) "Trump expects trade deal with UK to be completed 'very, very quickly'," *The Guardian*, 8 July, www.theguardian.com/world/2017/jul/08/theresa-may-in-bid-to-boost-post-brexit-trade-with-g20-meetings. Accessed 21 August 2017.

Barber, Tony (2016) "Five consequences of the UK's exit from the EU," *Financial Times*, 24 June, www.ft.com/content/b1a2d66e-3715–11e6–9a05–82a9b15a8ee7. Accessed 23 July 2017.

BBC (2014) "Profile: far-right Sweden Democrats," *BBC News: Europe*, 15 September, www.bbc.com/news/world-europe-29202793. Accessed 21 August 2017.

BBC (2016) "MH17 Ukraine plane crash: what we know," *BBC News: Europe*, 28 September, www.bbc.com/news/world-europe-28357880. Accessed 21 August 2017.

Bershidsky, Leonid (2017) "Turkey's troubled NATO status," *Bloomberg*, 14 March, www.bloomberg.com/view/articles/ 2017–03–14/turkey-s-nato-status-grows-more-troubled. Accessed 26 July 2017.

Bouillaud, Christophe (2016) "A long-term view on current Italian populism: Beppe Grillo's M5S (Five-Stars Movement) as the third wave of Italian populist upheaval," 2nd International Populism Conference, Prague, *Current Populism: Impact on the Political Landscape*, May.

Brands, Hal (2017) "The incompetence doctrine," War on the Rocks, 2 May, https://warontherocks.com/2017/05/the-incompetence-doctrine/. Accessed 21 August 2017.

Breslin-Smith, Janet (2016) "What Obama may find in Arabia next week: a sense of authority in crisis," *Foreign Policy*, 11 April. http://foreignpolicy.com/2016/04/11/what-obama-may-find-in-arabia-next-week-a-sense-of-authority-in-crisis/. Accessed 21 August 2017.

CFR (2014) "The Sunni-Shia divide," Council on Foreign Relations, www.cfr.org/interactives/sunni-shia-divide#!/. Accessed 17 August 2017.

Coffé, Hilde (2008) "Social Democratic parties as buffers against the extreme right: the case of Belgium," *Contemporary Politics*, 14:2, 179–95, doi:10.1080/13569770802176903.

Cohen, Marshall (2017) "Everything Trump has said about who tried to hack the US election," *CNN Politics*, 21 June, www.cnn.com/2017/06/21/politics/trump-russia-hacking-statements/index.html. Accessed 21 August 2017.

Cohen, Roger (2016) "The Trump possibility," *New York Times*, 3 October, www.nytimes.com/2016/10/04/opinion/the-trump-possibility.html?_r=0. Accessed 29 April 2017.

Cohn, Nate (2016) "Why the surprise over 'Brexit'? Don't blame the polls," *New York Times*, 24 June, www.nytimes.com/2016/06/25/upshot/why-the-surprise-over-brexit-dont-blame-the-polls.html?_r=0. Accessed 21 August 2017.

Colton, Timothy J. (2016) *Russia: What Everyone Needs To Know*, New York: Oxford University Press.

Dimitriadi, Angeliki (2016) "Deals without borders: Europe's foreign policy on migration," European Council on Foreign Affairs, April, www.ecfr.eu/publications/summary/deals_without_bor ders_europes_foreign_policy_on_migration6054. Accessed 21 July 2017.

Downs, William M. (2002) "How effective is the Cordon Sanitaire? Lessons from efforts to contain the far right in Belgium, France, Denmark, and Norway," *Journal für Konflikt- und Gewaltforschung/Journal of Conflict and Violence Research*, 4:1, 32–51, www.uni-bielefeld.de/ikg/jkg/1–2002/downs.pdf. Accessed 21 August 2017.

Dullien, Sebastian (2016) "Paying the price: the cost of Europe's refugee crisis," European Council on Foreign Relations, 28 April, www.ecfr.eu/publications/summary/paying_the_price_the_co st_of_europes_refugee_crisis. Accessed 10 July 2017.

Economist (2000) "Christoph Blocher, ascendant Swiss populist," *The Economist*, 17 August, www.economist.com/node/318248. Accessed 21 August 2017.

Economist (2017) "Aleksei Navalny's protesters are a force to be reckoned with," *The Economist*, 17 June, www.economist.com/ news/europe/21723439-anti-corruption-activist-chief-threat-vladimir-putin-next-years-election-aleksei. Accessed 4 July 2017.

Eissenstat, Howard and Cook, Steven A. (2017) "The massive protest putting Turkey's Erdogan on the offensive," *War on the Rocks*, 7 July, https://warontherocks.com/2017/07/the-massive-protest-putting-turkeys-erdogan-on-the-defensive/. Accessed 26 July 2017.

Emmott, Bill (2017) *The Fate of the West*, New York: Public Affairs.

Encarnación, Omar G. (2017) "The Spanish exception: why Spain has resisted right-wing populism," *Foreign Affairs*, 20 July, www.foreignaffairs.com/articles/spain/2017–07–20/spanish-excep tion. Accessed 1 August 2017.

EUROPA (2017) "The history of the European Union," *EUROPA*, Official Website of the European Union, 7 September, https:// europa.eu/european-union/about-eu/history_en. Accessed 21 August 2017.

Foulkes, Imogen (2014) "Swiss migration quotas: rift with EU grows," *BBC News: Europe*, 3 May, www.bbc.com/news/world-europe-27244959. Accessed 21 August 2017.

Gall, Carlotta (2017) "'March for Justice' ends in Istanbul with a pointed challenge to Erdogan," *New York Times*, 9 July, www.nytimes.com/2017/07/09/world/europe/turkey-march-for-justice-istanbul.html?_r=1. Accessed 26 July 2017.

Hall, Peter (2016) "The roots of Brexit: 1992, 2004, and European Union expansion," *Foreign Affairs*, 28 June, www.foreignaffairs.com/articles/united-kingdom/2016–06–28/roots-brexit. Accessed 21 August 2017.

Hawkins, K. A. (2010) *Venezuela's Chavismo and Populism in Comparative Perspective*, Cambridge: Cambridge University Press.

Heilbrunn, Jacob (2000) "A disdain for the past: Jörg Haider's Austria," *World Policy Journal*, 17:1, Spring, 71–78, doi:10.1215/07402775–2000–2011.

Hopkin, Jonathan (2016) "Brexit backlash: the populist rage fueling the referendum," *Foreign Affairs*, 21 June, www.foreignaffairs.com/articles/united-kingdom/2016–06–21/brexit-backlash. Accessed 21 August 2017.

Howard, Michael (1977) *War and the Liberal Conscience*, New Brunswick, NJ: Rutgers University Press.

Kalb, Marvin (2015) *Imperial Gamble: Putin, Ukraine, and the New Cold War*, Washington, DC: Brookings Institution.

Koenis, Jacques Paulus (2017) "A history of Dutch populism, from the murder of Pim Fortuyn to the rise of Geert Wilders," *Huffington Post*, 14 March, www.huffingtonpost.com/entry/a-history-of-dutch-populism-from-the-murder-of-pim_us_58c817a4e4b0d06aa658050e. Accessed 21 August 2017.

Lomax, Bill (2007) "The strange death of 'civil society' in post-communist Hungary," *Journal of Communist Studies and Transition Politics*, 13(1), 41–63, doi:10.1080/13523279708415331.

Mackintosh, Eliza (2017) "No more excuses on resettling refugees, European Commission warns," *CNN*, 2 March, www.cnn.com/2017/03/02/europe/european-countries-not-meeting-refugee-resettling-obligations/index.html. Accessed 10 July 2017.

Manchester, Julia (2017) "David Duke: Charlottesville protests about 'fulfilling promises of Donald Trump'," *The Hill*, 12 August, http://thehill.com/blogs/blog-briefing-room/news/346326-david-duke-charlottesville-protests-about-fulfilling-promises. Accessed 21 August 2017.

Marchetti, Silvia (2017) "How the Northern League's Matteo Salvini plans to bring Italy's far-right to power," *Time*, 26 January, http://time.com/4645415/matteo-salvini-italy-liga-nord/. Accessed 20 June 2017.

Marten, Kimberly (2017) *Reducing Tensions between Russia and NATO*, Council Special Report, Washington, DC: Center for Preventive Action, Council on Foreign Relations, March, www.cfr.org/report/reducing-tensions-between-russia-and-nato. Accessed 21 August 2017.

McBride, James (2017) "What Brexit means," Council on Foreign Affairs, 9 June, www.cfr.org/backgrounder/what-brexit-means. Accessed 21 August 2017.

Middle East Monitor (2017) "German troops to leave Turkey's Incirlik base in July," Middle East Monitor, 18 June, www.middleeastmonitor.com/20170618-german-troops-to-leave-turkeys-incirlik-base-in-july/. Accessed 26 July 2017.

Mindock, Clark (2017) "FBI director James Comey says Russia is 'greatest threat of any nation on earth'," *Independent*, 3 May, www.independent.co.uk/news/world/americas/us-politics/russia-james-comey-hearing-putin-greatest-threat-any-nation-earth-a7716016.html. Accessed 21 August 2017.

Monaghan, Andrew (2017) *Power in Modern Russia*, Manchester: Manchester University Press.

Mudde, Cas (2007) *Populist Radical Right Parties in Europe*, Cambridge: Cambridge University Press.

Mudde, Cas (2014) "Fighting the system? Populist radical right parties and party system change," *Party Politics*, 20:3, 3 February, 217–26, doi.org/10.1177/1354068813519968.

Müller, Jan-Werner (2016) *What is Populism?*, Philadelphia, PA: University of Pennsylvania Press.

Myers, Steven Lee (2016) *The New Tsar: The Rise and Reign of Vladimir Putin*, New York: Vintage Books/Random House LLC.

Ninkovich, Frank (2017) "Trumpism, history, and the future of U.S. foreign relations," The International Security Studies Forum Policy Series, 18 April, http://issforum.org/roundtables/poli cy/1–5AD-Ninkovich. Accessed 21 August 2017.

Ozturk, Ahmet Edi and Gözaydin, Iştar (2016) "Turkey's draft constitutional amendments: harking back to 1876," openDemocracy, 20 December, www.opendemocracy.net/ahmet-erdi-ozturk-tar-g-zayd-n/turkey-s-draft-constitutional-amendments-harking-ba ck-to-1876. Accessed 26 July 2017.

Pearson, W. Robert (2016) "Turkey invokes religion to restore influence," Middle East Institute, 18 April, http://www.mei.edu/con tent/article/turkey-invokes-religion-restore-influence. Accessed 26 July 2017.

Peterson, Nolan (2016) "2 years after airliner downed, eastern Ukraine remains a de facto no-fly zone," Daily Signal, 30 September, http://dailysignal.com/2016/09/30/2-years-after-air liner-downed-eastern-ukraine-remains-a-de-facto-no-fly-zone/. Accessed 21 August 2017.

Peterson, Scott (2017) "In Turkey, Erdoğan fans an Islamic nationalism to build Ottoman-style influence," Christian Science Monitor, 22 February, www.csmonitor.com/World/ Middle-East/2017/0222/In-Turkey-Erdogan-fans-an-Islamic-na tionalism-to-build-Ottoman-style-influence. Accessed 26 July 2017.

Pifer, Steven (2017) "Order from chaos: U.S.–Russian relations six months into the Trump administration," The Brookings Institution, 26 July. www.brookings.edu/blog/order-from-cha os/2017/07/26/u-s-russia-relations-six-months-into-the-tru mp-administration/?utm_campaign=Foreign%20Policy&utm _source=hs_email&utm_medium=email&utm_content=54 749962. Accessed 4 November 2017.

Ricks, Thomas E. (2017) Churchill & Orwell: The Fight for Freedom, New York: Penguin.

Salhani, Justin (2017) "Italy's populist movement isn't like the others in Europe. And that's worrisome," ThinkProgress, 18 May, https://thinkprogress.org/meet-the-italian-populist-right-c9fca24557f2/. Accessed 21 August 2017.

Shaheen, Kareem (2016) "Turkey coup attempt: Erdoğan declares three-month state of emergency," *The Guardian*, 21 July, www.theguardian.com/world/2016/jul/20/erdogan-bans-academics-from-travel-holds-first-post-coup-security-meeting-ankara-turkey. Accessed 26 July 2017.

Sloan, Stanley R. (2016) *Defense of the West: NATO, the European Union and the Transatlantic Bargain*, Manchester: Manchester University Press.

Sloan, Stanley R. (2017) "Policy series: Donald Trump and NATO: historic alliance meets a-historic president," H-Diplo International Security Studies Forum, 8 June, https://issforum.org/roundtables/policy/1–5AM-NATO. Accessed 21 August 2017.

Soros, George (2017) "Brexit in reverse?," Project Syndicate, 19 June, www.project-syndicate.org/commentary/brexit-in-reverse-by-george-soros-2017–06. Accessed 8 August 2017.

Soussi, Alasdair (2017) "The UK and US: the myth of the special relationship," *Al Jazeera*, 27 February, www.aljazeera.com/indepth/features/2017/02/uk-myth-special-relationship-170221082834995.html. Accessed 21 August 2017.

Stein, Aaron (2017) "'Take to the streets': Turkey's failed coup, one year later," *War on the Rocks*, 14 July, https://warontherocks.com/2017/07/take-to-the-streets-turkeys-failed-coup-one-year-later/. Accessed 26 July 2017.

Tait, Robert (2016) "Miloš Zeman: the hardline Czech leader fanning hostility to refugees," *The Guardian*, 14 September, www.theguardian.com/world/2016/sep/14/milos-zeman-czech-leader-refugees. Accessed 21 August 2017.

Traub, James (2016) "The party that wants to make Poland great again," *New York Times*, 2 November, www.nytimes.com/2016/11/06/magazine/the-party-that-wants-to-make-poland-great-again.html?mcubz=3&_r=0. Accessed 21 August 2017.

Trump, Donald J. (2016) "Trump on foreign policy," National Interest, 27 April, http://nationalinterest.org/feature/trump-foreign-policy-15960. Accessed 21 August 2017.

UK Electoral Commission (2016) "EU referendum results," UK Electoral Commission, www.electoralcommission.org.uk/

find-information-by-subject/elections-and-referendums/upco ming-elections-and-referendums/eu-referendum/electorate-and -count-information. Accessed 21 August 2017.

US Department of State (2014) "Ukraine and Russia sanctions," US Department of State, www.state.gov/e/eb/tfs/spi/ukrainerus sia/. Accessed 21 August 2017.

Versluis, Arthur (2016) "A conversation about radicalism in contemporary Greece," *Journal for the Study of Radicalism*, 10:1, Spring, 145–62, doi:10.14321/jstudradi.10.1.0145.

Wike, Richard, Stokes, Bruce, Pushter, Jacob, and Fetterolf, Janell (2017) "U.S. image suffers as publics around world question Trump's leadership," Pew Research Center, 26 June, www.pew global.org/2017/06/26/u-s-image-suffers-as-publics-around-wo rld-question-trumps-leadership/. Accessed 16 August 2017.

Wildman, Sarah (2007) "Dewinter's tale," *New Republic*, 21 January, https://newrepublic.com/article/62330/guess-whos-coming-se der-dewinters-tale. Accessed 21 August 2017.

Zalan, Eszter (2016) "Hungary is too small for Viktor Orban," *Foreign Policy*, 1 October, http://foreignpolicy.com/2016/10/01/ hungary-is-too-small-for-viktor-orban/. Accessed 22 June 2017.

Index